Joel Rifkin

The Horrifying & True Story of Joel The Ripper

**The Serial Killer Books
Volume 4**

By
Jack Rosewood
&
Rebecca Lo

ISBN-13:978-1986277037

Copyright © 2018 by LAK Publishing

ALL RIGHTS RESERVED

No part of this book may be reproduced, stored in a retrieval system, or transmitted in any form or by any means, electronic, mechanical, photocopying, recording, scanning, or otherwise, without the prior written permission of the publisher.

FREE BONUS!

Get two free books when you sign up to my VIP newsletter at
http://www.jackrosewood.com/free
150 interesting trivia facts about serial killers and the story of serial killer Herbert Mullin.

TABLE OF CONTENTS

Introduction 1

CHAPTER 1: Shaping of the Man 3

   From the Beginning 3

   Joel the Turtle 4

   Lonesome Teen 5

CHAPTER 2: From Fantasy to Reality 7

   A Troubled Young Man 7

   Passionate About Prostitutes 10

   Fantasy World 11

CHAPTER 3: The Deaths of Seventeen 13

   No Going Back 13

   Murders of Many 14

   The Last Hurrah 26

CHAPTER 4: It All Comes to an End 29

   Trooper's Shocking Discovery 29

   A Startling Confession 30

   Gathering of Evidence 32

CHAPTER 5: Justice is Served 34

   Rifkin on Trial..34

   Defending a Monster 36

   Further Trials 37

CHAPTER 6: Searching for Answers 42

   An Interesting Brain 42

   Classification and Method 48

   Dismemberment and Decomposition 52

CHAPTER 7: The Victims 57

   First to Die, Last to be Identified 57

   A Family Disagrees 58

   Timeline of Their Deaths..60

CHAPTER 8: More Questions than Answers 64

   Rifkin's Interviews 64

   Problems in Prison 67

   Appeals and Lawsuits...77

CHAPTER 9: Adopted Killers 79

   Adopted Child Syndrome 79

   Other Adopted Killers...86

   Fact or Fiction? 95

CHAPTER 10: Long Island Serial Killer? 100

   Background of the Case 100

- Rifkin Considered a Suspect 110
- Rifkin Talks About the Long Island Serial Killer 114

CHAPTER 11: Life vs. Death 117
- Pros and Cons 118
- Controversy 126

CHAPTER 12: The Impact of Movies and Rifkin Media 150
- Frenzy 150
- Cases of Murder Mimicking Media 152
- Items of Media Regarding Rifkin 157

Conclusion 162

More Books By Jack Rosewood 164

INTRODUCTION

Joel Rifkin, the quiet gardener, was a loner and a keeper of many dark and disturbing thoughts and secrets. He had committed the worst sin possible, slaughtering and dismembering his victims beneath his mother's own roof without being detected for about four years, until a simple lack of maintenance on his vehicle led to his discovery.

With a passionate obsession for prostitutes, Rifkin trolled the streets of Manhattan and Long Island at night, searching for working girls to satisfy his needs. Some he set free after indulging in sexual acts, but others were not so lucky. For seventeen women, they never got to go home again; they never got the opportunity to change their lives for the better. And for some, they have never been identified or found.

When state troopers pulled Rifkin over one night and discovered a body in the back of his truck, they knew they had caught a killer, but they couldn't imagine in all their wildest nightmares just how much of a killer Rifkin was. Immediately, he confessed he had killed seventeen prostitutes, with some being dismembered and thrown into the rivers nearby. These were the types of crimes they hoped they would never see or experience. And here was

Rifkin, happily dictating to them exactly what he had done with each victim.

Clearly, Rifkin is a very disturbed individual, but like many other serial killers, he wasn't insane. That's what makes the case so much more horrendous and difficult to understand. Nobody truly understands why Rifkin killed, what his motives were, or how it could have been prevented.

CHAPTER 1:

SHAPING OF THE MAN

From the Beginning

Rifkin entered the world on January 20, 1959, in New York, the result of a relationship between his 20-year-old birthmother and 24-year-old college student father. Unwanted by his birthparents, he was put up for adoption, and at three-weeks-old, he was taken home by his new parents, Benjamin Rifkin and his wife Jeanne.

The Rifkin's adopted another child three years later, a baby girl, and by 1965, the family of four had settled in the neighborhood of East Meadow, in Long Island, New York. Rifkin would spend most of his life in East Meadow, until he was incarcerated.

The family lived a normal life, with no reports of domestic troubles or abuse in the home. Rifkin's adoptive parents raised both of their children as if they were their own, and being an upper middle class family, there were no issues of poverty or other socioeconomic factors that would shape the mind of young Rifkin.

He was, however, a very shy child and fairly awkward around

other children. From the moment he enrolled in school, Rifkin's life became one of constant teasing, bullying, and abuse by his peers.

Joel the Turtle

Schooling for Rifkin was fraught with numerous issues right from the start. Despite having an IQ of 128, he suffered from learning disabilities—later believed to be dyslexia, but this was never diagnosed formally—and as a result he struggled academically.

A constant target of bullies, Rifkin was given the nickname 'Joel the Turtle' by his peers, largely because of the unusual way he walked with a 'sloping' posture and his slow pace. This also led to Rifkin being excluded from participating in sports because none of his peers wanted to choose him for their team.

The level of bullying against Rifkin was severe and went way beyond a bit of teasing and joking around. He never did anything to warrant the attacks by his peers; they just selected him as the target of their nastiness. He suffered daily at school, the brunt of horribly sadistic pranks and jokes, and regularly had his books and lunch stolen. Bullies would come up behind him and pull his pants down, and the bullying eventually escalated to a more violent nature, with Rifkin being assaulted regularly.

Rifkin became afraid of being in school and just as scared of being out of it. The abuse had gotten so bad that he would hang around after school, waiting until there were no signs of any of the other kids before walking home. He couldn't go outside and play in the neighborhood for fear of being picked on. It seemed that each time he stepped outside the house, he would be attacked verbally or physically.

Lonesome Teen

Upon Rifkin's attendance at East Meadow High School, things deteriorated even further. His grades were terrible, which his father found embarrassing, and he apparently yelled at Rifkin, asking him why he couldn't do anything to please his father. His mother, Jeanne, was fairly oblivious to the bullying Rifkin had been suffering and believed he was just a bit of a loner.

Already a target for bullies, Rifkin's own attire and manner made him even more of a soft touch at high school. He looked like the typical 'nerd' of that era with his pants pulled up high, his white socks showing above his shoes, and his glasses. One of the people who bullied Rifkin later referred to him as an 'abuse unit', that although he didn't do anything to bring about the unwanted attention, his sheer presence seemed to annoy people.

Rifkin tried to fit in with the other kids by joining the track team, but this was unsuccessful. He was taunted by a new nickname, 'lard ass', regularly had his head pushed into the toilet, and his clothes were often stolen and hidden from him. But Rifkin was determined to change things, and instead of fighting the bullies, he invited them around to his house to drink beer and watch television. Unbeknownst to Rifkin, he was just being used, and they had no intention of befriending him.

Because he had been unsuccessful at athletics, Rifkin decided to join the yearbook staff. Straight away, someone stole his camera, but he didn't give up. He worked diligently to get the yearbook out on time but was devastated when he was left out of the wrap-up party held to celebrate. He graduated in 1977, at the bottom of the class, but he hoped that life would get better once he went to college.

CHAPTER 2:

FROM FANTASY TO REALITY

A Troubled Young Man

Rifkin had attempted to date girls while he was still at high school, but thanks to his bullies, he was unable to even get through the first dates. Unable to even successfully complete the first of his date pursuits. On one occasion, he had arranged to go out with a girl, but some of the track team athletes had other plans. They trapped him in the school gym and threw eggs at him, and Joel had to call his father.

The second time Rifkin tried to go on a date, the bullies foiled his plan once again. This time, Rifkin and his date had managed to make it to a pizza parlor before being seen, but it didn't last. The bullies found them and chased them both, running after them down the street until Rifkin and his date were able to hide in the local library. By the time he started college, Rifkin had not maintained a relationship, much less asked anyone to be his girlfriend, or experienced a real romance.

His first year of college was spent at Nassau Community College, located on Long Island. He found it all rather boring, and he had a habit of cutting his classes. By the end of the first year, he had only managed to complete one course.

In the fall of 1978, he transferred to SUNY Brockport, the State University of New York at Brockport, a suburb of Rochester, and here he joined the photography club. Rifkin finally developed a relationship with a girl, but it didn't go anywhere because she claimed he was a sweet guy but was depressed all the time.

Unfortunately, his academic performance was poor, and he ended up dropping out of college in 1980. He moved back with his parents and decided to attend Nassau Community College again. His pattern of cutting classes continued, and he was seldom there, so he finally left for the last time in 1984.

Out of school, Rifkin worked a variety of jobs but didn't last very long at any of them. Like at college, he constantly was absent from work, his hygiene levels were poor, and he seemed to be inept at doing the simplest of tasks. One former employer even claimed Rifkin couldn't count to ten.

When he wasn't working, Rifkin daydreamed a lot about one day becoming a poet or a famous writer, but any attempts to write always resulted in bleak or dark content. He was still interested in horticulture and photography but hadn't been successful at developing either hobby into a paying job. Rifkin moved out several times but always returned to his parents' home when he lost a job.

In the fall of 1986, Rifkin's father Benjamin was already suffering from emphysema when he was diagnosed with cancer of the prostate. Chronically ill and in a lot of pain, Benjamin decided to end his suffering by overdosing on barbiturates in February 1987. He lay in a coma for four days before passing away. At the funeral, Rifkin brought the mourners to tears with the eulogy for his father, and his own depression worsened.

The following year, Rifkin attended the State College of Technology in New York to study a two-year horticulture program. Incredibly, he earned straight A's for two semesters, which resulted in him being chosen for an internship at Planting Fields Arboretum, located in Oyster Bay.

It was a huge honor for Rifkin to be selected for the internship, and he was even more delighted to discover one of the other interns was a pretty blonde girl. He was attracted to her and would 'shadow' her whenever he could, but he wasn't brave enough to ask her out on a date. In his mind though, they were engaged in a fantasy affair. Rifkin became hugely frustrated when she showed no signs of being interested in him, and he had now reached his breaking point.

Childhood Timeline

1959 - Born in New York and adopted at three weeks of age.
1962 - Second child, a girl, adopted and named Jan.
1965 - Rifkin started to collect items such as limestone, basalt, coal, sandstone and clay.

1967 - Began taking an interest in photography and handcrafts.

1970 - Rifkin is told by his parents that he was adopted.

1977 - First time Rifkin had sexual intercourse, at the age of 18.

1984 - Attended Nassau Community College and later dropped out.

1987 - Rifkin's father commits suicide by an overdose of barbiturates.

Passionate About Prostitutes

Rifkin had a fascination and preoccupation with prostitutes which had begun back in 1972. He first got the idea of strangling prostitutes after watching Frenzy, an Alfred Hitchcock film. It wasn't long after this that his parents purchased him a car, and he was able to drive around the streets at night trolling for prostitutes.

His use of prostitutes increased when he was attending Nassau Community College, and a lot of the times when he failed to attend classes, it was because he was indulging himself with a prostitute. The same was happening when he was absent from his jobs. He preferred spending his time with prostitutes, rather than working or attending classes.

Rifkin spent so much money on prostitutes that he ended up in debt. However, not all of his experiences with the ladies of the night were good. There were times when he was robbed by the prostitutes and sometimes even their pimps. One particular woman managed to rob him on two occasions, using the same ruse, and got away with it.

On August 22, 1987, Rifkin made the mistake of trying to solicit sex from the wrong woman. She turned out to be an undercover police officer, and he was arrested and fined. He was able to hide his arrest from his mother and decided he would have to go further afield to pick up prostitutes so she would never know what he was up to.

Rifkin began seeking prostitutes in Manhattan, and at the same time he started to collect newspaper articles on serial killers, mainly those who murdered prostitutes. Many of these were about killer Arthur Shawcross and the Green River Killer, who at that time was unidentified. Initially, he told himself he was studying them, but in reality, he was preparing to emulate them.

Fantasy World

The intense loneliness of Rifkin's childhood and early adulthood had led him to withdraw into his own world. For years he had been fantasizing about raping women and stabbing them to death. Even though he daydreamed about strangling prostitutes, he was yet to carry out his fantasy despite his dalliances with numerous prostitutes.

Every minute Rifkin wasn't with a prostitute, he was fantasizing about killing them. The years of abuse and mistreatment he had suffered, coupled with his feelings of loneliness, were taking a serious toll on his mental health. He was filled with thoughts and feelings of violence and rage, and he was basically a ticking time bomb, fighting the urges every day.

Rifkin had finally reached his breaking point in March 1989. The terrible mental fantasies were not going away, and he could no longer ignore them. He had created a plan, waited until his mother went away on a business trip, and then went looking for a prostitute.

CHAPTER 3:

THE DEATHS OF SEVENTEEN

No Going Back

In the first week of March 1989, Rifkin had made the decision to kill a prostitute. He had been dreaming of it for so long, and for some reason he decided it was time. After his mother left for her trip, he picked up a young woman called Susie in Manhattan's East Village.

According to Rifkin, Susie was a serious drug addict, and they made a few stops to purchase drugs on the way back to his house. They had intercourse, which he described as 'listless', then Susie asked if they could go back out and get more drugs. At this point, Rifkin picked up a howitzer shell that his parents kept as a souvenir and struck her with it multiple times. He only stopped when he became too tired to continue.

But Susie wasn't dead, and when Rifkin tried to shift her, she bit him on the finger rather deeply. He then strangled her to death. Rifkin managed to get her body into a trash bag and went about cleaning the living room of blood and chaos. He then lay down for several hours to rest.

When Rifkin woke, he dragged Susie to the basement of the house and laid her body across the washer and dryer. Using a craft knife, he dismembered the body and used pliers to remove her teeth so she couldn't be identified. He also cut off her fingertips so no prints remained with which to identify her.

Rifkin shoved Susie's dismembered head into an empty paint can and put the rest of her body parts into trash bags before loading it all into his mother's car. He drove to New Jersey and dumped the legs and head in woodland near Hopewell, and as he returned to Manhattan, he tossed the rest of the body parts into the East River.

He hadn't been as clever as he thought however, and it was only a few days before Susie's head was discovered. A gentleman playing golf at the Hopewell Valley Golf Club made the shocking discovery on March 5 after searching the woods for a wayward golf ball. Despite her head being found, police were unable to identify her at the time, but they were able to determine that she was HIV positive, and when the news was broadcast, Rifkin had a major panic attack due to the possibility he may have been infected.

Murders of Many

Julie Blackbird

It was over a year before Rifkin killed again. Although the dates aren't exact, it was sometime in late 1990 when he struck again.

This time, he chose his victim because he thought she looked a little like the music star, Madonna. His victim was Julie Blackbird, another prostitute.

His mother was out of town again, and Rifkin took Julie back to the house where they spent the night together. The following morning, Rifkin grabbed a heavy wooden table leg and beat Julie with it, then strangled her to death. He later admitted that he considered having sex with her corpse like Ted Bundy had done but found the thought too repulsive.

With Julie's body still in the house, Rifkin went out and bought a mortar pan and some cement, determined there would be no chance of her body being found like Susie's had been. As like before, he dismembered Julie's body and put her head, legs, and arms in buckets before filling them with cement. Her torso was placed into a milk crate and also filled with cement.

Rifkin disposed of the torso and head in the East River in Manhattan and then threw the rest of the body parts into a barge canal in Brooklyn. Her remains were never found, but her death was detailed by Rifkin during his confession. Police discovered her personal diary among Rifkin's possessions.

Barbara Jacobs

Rifkin picked up 31-year-old Barbara on the evening of July 13, 1991, she was working as a prostitute. Barbara was a drug addict and had been arrested previously on charges of prostitution and car theft. On returning to Rifkin's home, they had sexual intercourse and Barbara fell asleep. Seizing the opportunity, Rifkin picked up a table leg, the same he had used to bludgeon Julie Blackbird, and struck her in the head with it. He then proceeded to strangle her with his bare hands until she was dead.

Rifkin wasn't keen on dismembering another body, as he found the task repulsive, so he developed another method for disposing of Barbara's body. He wrapped her up in plastic and then stowed her in a large cardboard box, folding her body up so she would fit. After putting the box into the back of his mother's pickup truck, Rifkin drove to the Hudson River and dropped the box into the water before driving back home.

This wasn't as successful as his previous methods, however, as Barbara's remains were found just hours later. A group of firefighters happened to be on a training exercise in that area and located the box with Barbara's body inside near a cement plant. Initially, her cause of death was deemed a drug overdose by the coroner, but Rifkin confessed to her murder when under questioning after his arrest two years later.

Until his confession, the body had remained unidentified, and Barbara had been buried in Potter's Field cemetery as a Jane Doe. Rifkin claimed that when her body was initially discovered, he wasn't concerned as he didn't think anyone would link the body back to him. It appears that he was no longer fearful of his victims being found.

Mary Ellen DeLuca

Mary Ellen DeLuca, 22, was working as a prostitute to feed her drug habit when she crossed paths with Rifkin on September 1, 1991. That night, she had been with a group of friends but needed her next fix of crack, so she willingly got into Rifkin's vehicle. Instead of going straight back to his house, this time they drove around New York until the sun came up, stopping at various places to purchase drugs.

By the time they arrived at a cheap motel, Rifkin had already spent around $150 on drugs, but Mary was still demanding more. She wasn't keen on having sex since she had gotten her fix anyway, but she eventually agreed to go through with it. However, she tried to rush the whole process and complained the whole time, angering Rifkin. At one point amid the complaints, he asked Mary if she wanted to die, and according to his account, she said yes.

Rifkin began strangling Mary, and he said she did nothing to try and fight it, instead accepting that she was going to die. He later said that this murder was a 'weird one', most likely because of the way she reacted as he was strangling her, almost as if he was doing her a favor.

But now Rifkin had a big problem—how to get her dead body out of the motel without being seen. It was now daylight, and he wasn't at home where he had more options of disposal. So, remembering a scene from his favorite movie 'Frenzy', he went out and purchased a steamer trunk. He managed to force Mary's body into the trunk and get it out to his vehicle. He then drove to Orange County, pulled into a rest stop just outside of Cornwall, and left the trunk there. He made no attempt to cover or camouflage the trunk at all, obviously not concerned about it being found quickly.

Remarkably, the trunk with Mary's body contained inside wasn't found until a month later, on October 1. There was no ID in the trunk, and she was naked except for her bra. By now, the body had decomposed quite dramatically, and the coroner was unable to determine how she had died. Like Barbara Jacobs, Mary was also buried as a Jane Doe and wasn't identified until June 1993.

Yun Lee

Rifkin's obsession with prostitutes didn't slow down, but not all of them met their fate at his hands. He continued to pick up prostitutes after he murdered Mary Ellen DeLuca, but he let them go without harm. In fact, his next victim was actually the second prostitute he had picked up one September night, and she would not be so fortunate.

Yun Lee was a 31-year-old Korean prostitute that Rifkin had picked up on previous occasions. She agreed to go with him, but when they started having sex, Rifkin was unable to perform, possibly because he had already been with another prostitute that night. Whatever the reason for his inadequacy, he struck Yun Lee then strangled her. During the strangulation, she allegedly mouthed to him that he was making a big mistake.

This was the first time Rifkin had murdered someone he had already known, and he later stated that he felt a fleeting sense of remorse at her death. But it was short-lived, and his next plan of action was to dispose of her body. Using a similar steamer trunk as the one he had used to get rid of Mary's body, he managed to fit Yun Lee's body into it and then disposed of it in the East River. Her remains were discovered on September 23, several days before Mary Ellen DeLuca's body was found, despite the latter woman being murdered first. This time, Yun Lee was identified by her ex-husband, so she was able to be buried under her name instead of as a Jane Doe.

Number Six

Just before Christmas Day in 1991, Rifkin picked up a prostitute on West 46th Street, Manhattan, but was unable to recall her name. While she was performing oral sex on him in his vehicle, he strangled her, and according to Rifkin later, she died a quick death. Leaving her body in the passenger seat, he drove her to his workplace and hid the body under a tarpaulin.

Rifkin then drove to Westbury, to a recycling plant he once worked at, and picked up a 55-gallon drum that had once been used to hold oil. He went back to where the body was hidden and placed her into the drum. His next stop was an area of junkyards in the South Bronx, and he rolled the drum into the East River, thinking it would remain unnoticed amid all the other junk piled around.

Remarkably, as he was about to leave the scene, he was stopped by police who accused him of dumping rubbish illegally. He managed to convince them that he had been collecting junk rather than dumping it, and they warned him and let him go.

Rifkin found the drum had worked so well that he decided to use them for future victims. He purchased several more of the drums.

Lorraine Orvieto

Lorraine Orvieto, 28, suffered from manic depression, and instead of taking medication, she used cocaine to try and control her mood swings. Her use of the drug was costly, and she had been working as a prostitute to make the money she needed to fund her habit. Rifkin was driving around in Bay Shore, Long Island, on December 26, 1991, when he came across Lorraine and propositioned her. She agreed to go with him and they drove to a nearby school.

Rifkin parked his vehicle next to a fence by the school and Lorraine began performing oral sex on him. Rifkin proceeded to strangle her to death, and upon inspection of the contents in her purse after her demise, he discovered she was HIV-positive. He decided to keep her AZT medicine as well as her jewelry and her ID, trophies of the murder.

He drove back to his landscaping workplace and stuffed Lorraine's body into one of the oil drums. Then, he drove to Brooklyn and dropped the drum into Coney Island Creek. It was found on July 11, 1992, by a fisherman, and at that point her own family hadn't even filed a missing person's report. It was another two months before anybody bothered to report that she was missing.

Mary Ann Holloman

Rifkin's need to kill was escalating, and the time between murders was getting shorter. Just a week after killing Lorraine Orvieto, he was out hunting for his next victim. Unfortunately for Mary Ann Holloman, she crossed his path on January 2, 1992. Mary, 39, was a drug-addicted prostitute who did a bit of sewing for local strippers as a sideline income source. She would be Rifkin's oldest victim.

After Rifkin picked up Mary, he took her to the same parking lot where he had taken Yun Lee the night he killed her. While Mary was performing oral sex on Rifkin, he strangled her to death. During his confessions later on, he couldn't recall any remarkable memories or thoughts about this murder. He drove her body back to Long Island and shoved it into an oil drum before dumping it in the Coney Island Creek.

The drum containing Mary's body was found on July 9, 1992, following a report from an anonymous caller. Mary was identified by dental records, and her body was taken by her family to be buried. Two days after her body had been found, the drum containing Lorraine Orvieto was discovered. It was now clear to the authorities that there was possibly a serial killer at work, but with an overwhelming number of murders to deal with each year and prostitutes not being considered high priority, Rifkin was able to continue on.

Number Nine

Although considered to be Rifkin's ninth victim, this unidentified woman was found before the previous two victims. Rifkin was unable to summon up a great deal about this victim and had no idea what her name had been. All he was able to remember was that he had picked her up in Manhattan and that she had tattoos. Also, that she had fought hard for her life when he strangled her.

This victim was placed into Rifkin's last oil drum and dropped into Newtown Creek in Brooklyn. On May 13, 1992, the drum was discovered floating with the current, and on closer inspection, a foot could be seen protruding through the rusty metal of the drum. Toxicology tests performed subsequent to the autopsy identified a large quantity cocaine in her system, which resulted in detectives mistakenly assuming she had been a drug mule who had accidentally died after a drug-filled condom had ruptured. It wasn't until Rifkin confessed that they realized how wrong they had been.

Iris Sanchez

On a day in April 1992, Rifkin had decided to skip work for the day and go cruising for some trouble instead. His idea of trouble was very different from that of most people though; he was looking for a prostitute. He found Iris Sanchez, 25, working the street on First Avenue, most likely trying to raise enough money to feed her crack habit.

After picking up Iris, he drove her to a housing project in Manhattan and they started to engage in sex. During the act, Rifkin strangled her and then drove across the Brooklyn Bridge with her body in the vehicle, looking for somewhere to dispose of her. He found an illegal dump located off Rockaway Boulevard, and after removing her jewelry, he shoved her beneath a rotting mattress. Despite the site being visible from JFK International Airport, nobody found her body until Rifkin drew a map for detectives after his arrest.

Anna Lopez

On Memorial Day, May 25, 1992, Anna Lopez was working as a prostitute on Atlantic Avenue in Queens. Although she had three children at home, to three different fathers, she worked as a prostitute mainly because she was addicted to cocaine. On this particular day, Rifkin approached her and she agreed to go with him to a nearby residential street for sex in his vehicle.

Rifkin strangled Anna in the vehicle then drove all through the night to find the right spot to dispose of her body. He drove to Brewster, Putnam County, and dumped her body beside the I-84 freeway. She was found the following day by a motorist who had stopped to urinate. One of her earrings was later found in Rifkin's bedroom.

Violet O'Neill

When Rifkin picked up his next victim, Violet O'Neill, 21, he returned to his original methods of killing and disposal. He took prostitute Violet back to the home he shared with his mother in East Meadow. After they had sex, he strangled her to death before placing her in the bathtub and dismembering her body. He used black plastic to wrap up her torso, and her limbs were put into a suitcase. All of the body parts were then tossed into the Hudson River.

Mary Catherine Williams

The story of Mary Catherine Williams was a prime example of how a person's life can be completely turned around for the worse. Once a cheerleader at college and a homecoming queen, Mary moved to New York following the end of her marriage to try and develop a career in acting. Instead, she ended up addicted to drugs and homeless, working as a prostitute to pay for her drugs.

Rifkin and Mary had 'dated' a couple of times before, so she wouldn't have hesitated when he propositioned her again on October 2, 1992. He purchased some drugs for her, and when she fell asleep in the car, he tried to strangle her, but she woke up. She started fighting Rifkin, trying to save herself, but he overpowered her and smothered her to death.

He drove her body to Yorktown, Westchester, and left her there. He kept her purse, credit cards, and a large amount of costume jewelry she had in the purse. Her body was found on December 21, and like many others, she remained unidentified until Rifkin confessed.

Jenny Soto

The last victim of Rifkin in 1992 was Jenny Soto, 23. Jenny was an addict, and despite several trips to detox she was never able to kick the habit. On November 16, she was working the street near the Williamsburg Bridge in lower Manhattan when Rifkin pulled up and solicited her for sex. She agreed.

After Jenny and Rifkin had sex in his pickup truck, he strangled her, but she fought tooth and nail until the bitter end. She fought so hard that every one of her fingernails was broken as she clawed against his face and neck, desperately trying to break free. He later said she was the 'toughest one to kill'.

Rifkin kept her ID cards, earrings, underwear, and drug syringe as trophies to add to his growing collection. He then rolled her body into the Harlem River, very close to the spot where the remains of Yun Lee had been found over a year earlier. Jenny's body was found the next day and was identified by fingerprints.

This was the first time a victim had left marks on Rifkin where anyone could see them, and this shook him a bit. He had to try and explain how he had received the scratches, which unsettled him. This event slowed down his killing spree, and it would be 15 weeks before he struck again.

The Last Hurrah

It was now 1993, and Rifkin had experienced a fairly significant cooling off period since his last kill. He had taken this time to try and formulate better plans to prevent detection and to avoid situations where he would be injured as he had been during the murder of Jenny Soto.

Leah Evens

The first woman to die by Rifkin in 1993 was Leah Evens, 28. A single mother of two children, Leah was living in Brooklyn with her mother and had developed a drug habit. She worked as a prostitute to pay for her drugs and was working on the night of February 27 when Rifkin came across her.

Rifkin and Leah drove to an abandoned parking lot for sex, but after she started to undress, she changed her mind and demanded they find a place more private. Rifkin refused her demands, and when she started crying, he strangled her. He then drove to an area of woods in Long Island and buried her in a shallow grave, the only victim he buried.

Her body was found on May 9 by hikers, who noticed a hand sticking up out of the ground. Police were unable to identify the body and hired a forensic anthropologist to create a facial reconstruction. However Rifkin confessed to the crime before this was completed, and Leah's driver's license was found in his bedroom.

Lauren Marquez

Rifkin's next victim was another drug addicted prostitute. Lauren Marquez, 28, had moved to New York from Tennessee previously, and on April 2, 1993, she was working as a prostitute on Second Avenue when Rifkin picked her up.

After driving to an area near the Manhattan Bridge, Rifkin began to strangle her until he was distracted by a man walking his dog past the car. Lauren seized the opportunity to fight back and very nearly succeeded in escaping, but it wasn't to be, as Rifkin broke her neck. He disposed of her body in Suffolk County, and she remained undiscovered until he confessed.

Tiffany Bresciani

Tiffany Bresciani was the final victim of Rifkin. Originally from Louisiana, she had moved to New York with hopes of getting into dancing or acting. Unfortunately, she became addicted to heroin instead, and worked in strip clubs when not on the streets as a prostitute.

In the early hours of June 24, 1993, Rifkin picked up Tiffany, despite having already been with another prostitute that night. In fact, she was his fourth prostitute in just two days, such was his obsession. He drove Tiffany to the parking lot of the New York Post and strangled her to death. Leaving her body in the backseat of his mother's car, he drove back to his home, stopping to buy some rope and a tarpaulin to use for disposing of the body.

By the time Rifkin arrived home, Tiffany's body had been wrapped, tied, and placed into the trunk of his mother's car. As soon as he walked into the house, his mother demanded her keys and went out on a shopping trip, unaware there was a dead body in her trunk. Rifkin hadn't had time to shift it before his mother left.

After she returned, and still oblivious to the presence of the body, Rifkin shifted Tiffany into the garage and left her in a wheelbarrow among the clutter. Strangely, he spent the next three days working on his own pickup truck with the body still in the garage, despite the sweltering heat of summer and the stench of decomposing tissue.

He finally decided it was time to shift the body and loaded it into his pickup truck. He planned to dump it near Melville's Republic Airport, located about 15 miles away from his house, until a simple lack of vehicle maintenance brought him to the attention of police troopers.

CHAPTER 4:

IT ALL COMES TO AN END

Rifkin had been able to get away with so many murders without attracting even the slightest bit of suspicion that he became both arrogant and reckless. But all of that was to come to an end in June 1993, thanks to a missing license plate on his truck.

Trooper's Shocking Discovery

On the night of June 28, 1993, Rifkin was driving around with the body of Tiffany Bresciani in the back of his truck on his way to dispose of her remains when he caught the attention of state troopers. They noticed there were no license plates on his truck and attempted to pull Rifkin over, but he refused to stop.

What ensued was a rather bizarre type of police chase. Normally these chases would involve high speeds, but Rifkin never exceeded 50 mph throughout the chase. After 20 minutes of trying to escape, Rifkin crashed his truck into a utility pole. Ironically, it was right outside the courthouse in Mineola, New York.

The troopers cautiously approached the crashed vehicle and ordered Rifkin out, whereby they immediately placed him in handcuffs, as they would with any other fleeing driver. But it was then that one of the troopers noticed a foul odor coming from the back of Rifkin's truck. By the light of a flashlight, the trooper peeled back a corner of the blue tarpaulin and made a horrific discovery.

With Tiffany's corpse revealed, Rifkin knew the game was up, and he admitted to the troopers that she had been a prostitute and he had killed her. What had begun as a simple attempted traffic stop had turned into what would become one of the most notorious serial murder cases in American history.

A Startling Confession

When Rifkin made the first confession to the state troopers who apprehended him, they later recalled that his reaction and emotion while admitting the murder was cold. He told them he had picked her up near the Williamsburg Bridge, strangled her, and then hid the body for three days. He had been on his way to Republic Airport to dispose of the corpse when they caught him.

Rifkin was taken to Troop L Barracks for further investigation and questioning. What proceeded was around eight hours of Rifkin confessing to 17 murders, telling the investigators about each murder one at a time, like retelling a story. In some cases he could only remember small details about the women, but he recalled all of the factors around the murders and the disposal of the bodies.

Astonishingly, there were no recordings made of the interrogation, which lead to conflicting information regarding whether or not Rifkin was offered legal counsel. He later claimed he had asked for a lawyer multiple times but was told that he couldn't speak with a lawyer until he gave them more information. However, the written transcript tells a different story. It claims he was asked if he wanted a lawyer and Rifkin had said no.

The information Rifkin provided about each murder was very specific, including that he preferred women who were white, Asian, or Latino. He went into great detail about dismembering some of the bodies and where he had either dumped them or, in one case, buried them. Each story he told was done so in a matter-of-fact way, with little or no emotion. In some cases, he couldn't remember the name of a victim, but he could tell the officers what jewelry or clothing she had been wearing.

At first the investigators were uncertain how truthful Rifkin's stories were. They knew without a doubt he had killed at least one woman, considering her body was still in the back of his truck. But they couldn't be sure if he was recalling memories or stories he had read in books or newspapers.

When he told the investigators he had been 'using' prostitutes since the day he got his driver's license at the age of 16, they were horrified at the potential number of victims he may have killed. Because of his statements and the propensity for a high number of victims, investigators had to take what he was telling them seriously. He claimed to have dumped three bodies in South Hampton, so a team of investigators were sent there first.

Gathering of Evidence

While teams of investigators searched for bodies, warrants were also obtained to search Rifkin's vehicle, the home he still shared with his mother and any other places they could link him to. During these searches a vast number of evidentiary items were discovered.

At his home in East Meadow, his mother Jeanne was confronted with the sight of police officers outside her house. They initially told her Rifkin had been detained following a traffic incident, then that he was in jail for a crime, but they refused to tell her what the crime was. Later she saw a media report about her son and called Robert Sale, a criminal attorney, for assistance.

In Rifkin's bedroom, officers found numerous items belonging to women, including underwear, jewelry, purses and wallets, clothing, hair accessories, and makeup. They also found prescription medication packages with women's names on them and driver's licenses. There were a variety of photographs of women as well.

A lot of the items found in Rifkin's bedroom were later connected to cases of unsolved murders involving women. He had kept these items as trophies from each kill, a common behavior among serial killers. They serve as a tool for remembering each murder and the women they have killed.

Also found in the bedroom were a lot of books about various serial killers. It seemed as though Rifkin had been studying these killers, though at the time, it wasn't certain if he idolized them or was trying to understand his own mind. There were also pornographic movies, all with a sadistic tone to them.

The most disturbing discoveries were made in the garage of his home. In the wheelbarrow, investigators discovered three ounces of human blood. There were a number of tools that were also covered in human blood. On examining a chainsaw, the blades were found to contain both blood and human flesh stuck in them. There was no doubt at all that at least some of Rifkin's claims about committing multiple murders were true.

While investigators were searching for physical evidence, Rifkin was still confessing to his crimes. He wrote down a list of dates, names, and locations of his murder victims. Although some of the information was incomplete, investigators were able to piece together what Rifkin gave them, the evidence they had found, and missing person's reports to establish the identity of some of the victims.

CHAPTER 5:

JUSTICE IS SERVED

Criminal Attorney Robert Sale was contacted by Rifkin's mother to represent him for the murder charges on the same day the police searched the house. His first job was to contact the state police and insist they stop interrogating Rifkin until he could talk to him. Apparently though, they ignored this and continued to interview Rifkin for another hour or so. From their point of view, they had this horrendous murderer in custody, and they needed to do whatever it took to get as much information as they could out of him.

Rifkin on Trial

Rifkin and Sale met for the first time on the morning of June 29. At that time, Rifkin claimed to have a migraine headache because the police had taken his spectacles away from him, and he was barely able to function.

Half an hour later, Rifkin made his first appearance before Judge John Kingston to enter a plea regarding the murder of Tiffany Bresciani. He entered a plea of not guilty, and knowing it was futile to try for bond, Sale waived the bond application. There was no way they were going to let Rifkin out on bond.

Sale was able to get a postponement of the formal arraignment for two weeks, and Rifkin was sent to the Nassau County Correctional Facility located in East Meadow. Ironically, the trip took him right past the very high school where he had suffered so badly as a teen.

While awaiting trial, Rifkin decided to change his lawyer. He fired Sale and hired John Lawrence and Michael Soshnick. A former district attorney for Nassau County, Soshnick had an esteemed reputation in criminal law. His partner Lawrence however had no experience at the time in criminal law, but the two men worked well together.

In November 1993, the suppression hearing began, and the first thing Soshnick attempted was to try and get Rifkin's confession suppressed on the grounds that the arresting state troopers had not had probable cause to search his truck in the first place. This, of course, was denied.

Several weeks into the hearing, the prosecution offered Rifkin a plea deal. In exchange for a guilty plea for the 17 murders, he was offered 46 years to life. However, Rifkin was sure that he could dodge all of the charges with an insanity defense, so he declined the offer.

The hearing lasted for four months, during which time Rifkin's lawyer Soshnick repeatedly upset the presiding judge. He often arrived late to court and sometimes didn't make an appearance at all. For many scheduled appearances when Soshnick showed up, he was unprepared for court so Judge Wexner eventually ended the hearing in March, declaring there was enough evidence for him to reject the motions put forward by the defense and the trial date was set for April.

Rifkin infuriated by the result and Soshnick's representation fired him as his lawyer. He did, however, keep Lawrence on as his lawyer despite him having no experience in criminal trials. When the trial began on April 11, 1994, Rifkin went ahead with his plea of not guilty by reason of temporary insanity.

Defending a Monster

Opening arguments began on April 20, following the selection of five women and seven men for the jury. The prosecution described Rifkin as being a sexual sadist, a killer who enjoyed watching his victims suffer. Fred Klein stated, "He got caught red-handed, and now he's using and abusing the concept of mental illness."

In response, Lawrence argued that Rifkin was a "paranoid schizophrenic who lived in the twilight zone." He further insisted that Rifkin's compulsions to violently kill were overwhelming and that they had taken over his life. Throughout the prosecution's case, Rifkin snored, and when questioned about his behavior, Lawrence said Rifkin had an allergic reaction to a sandwich he ate.

Barbara Kirwin, a psychiatrist from Long Island, assessed Rifkin and testified that his psychological tests were the most pathological she had ever seen in the 20 years she had been a practicing psychiatrist. The prosecution brought forward Dr. Park Dietz to testify, who had previously been a state's witness in the cases against murderers Jeffrey Dahmer, Arthur Shawcross, and John Hinckley. He disagreed with Kirwin and stated that Rifkin was sick, but he wasn't insane. Dietz explained that Rifkin had known exactly what he was doing at the time of the murders.

Once both sides of the case had finished being presented, it was up to the jury to decide whether to accept Rifkin was insane at the time of the murders or not. There was no question that he had killed them, it was simply a matter of whether he knew what he was doing at the time.

On May 9, the jury deliberated briefly before returning with their decision. They declared Rifkin guilty of murder and reckless endangerment, the lesser charge for the police chase that ended with his arrest. Judge Wexner sentenced Rifkin to 25 years to life for the murder and up to seven years for the reckless endangerment.

Further Trials

Before his sentencing had even been handed down for the first trial, Rifkin was transferred to Suffolk County on May 9 to stand trial for the murders of Lauren Marquez and Leah Evens. Rifkin had hired a new lawyer, Martin Efman, and once again he entered an insanity plea as his defense. But this time, rather than focusing on the alleged schizophrenia proposed in the first trial, they had come up with a new 'disorder'.

Rifkin and his lawyer claimed that the trauma of being adopted had made him mentally ill, a condition called 'Adopted-Child Syndrome'. This illness was the result of a great deal of work by psychologist Dr. David Kirschner, and he agreed to be a witness for the defense team.

The prosecution argued that Adopted-Child Syndrome was really just an expression of an old belief that there was supposedly a link between violence and adoption. It is neither recognized as a legitimate mental disorder by the American Psychological Association, nor is it listed in the Diagnostic and Statistical Manual of Mental Disorders.

Efman contended that Rifkin being separated from his birthmother was so traumatic for him that he uncontrollably struck back at women he identified as being like his mother. Rifkin had previously claimed that his birthmother had been a prostitute who was too poor to afford an abortion, so she went through with the pregnancy and gave him up for adoption.

Dr. Kirschner believed that the separation Rifkin experienced from his birthmother led to him fantasizing about picking up prostitutes and murdering them, doing so in a dissociative state induced by the illness of Adopted-Child Syndrome.

During Rifkin's first trial, Dr. Kirschner had proposed they use this as his defense, but his lawyer at the time, Lawrence, wanted to instead focus on the schizophrenic defense. Dr. Kirschner had been treating adopted children for 26 years, and during that time he had discovered a pattern of behaviors including sexual promiscuity, stealing, and pathological lying. There were emotional disturbances as well, including anxiety, extreme antisocial behavior, and an absence of feeling guilty.

Dr. Kirschner had been involved in a dozen cases where adopted children had later gone on to commit murders. This doesn't happen with all cases of adopted children however, but was apparent in approximately 10% of children who were adopted. This led Dr. Kirschner to label it as a syndrome.

At the trial, Judge John J.J. Jones Jr. presided, and dismissed claims by Rifkin that his constitutional right to have a lawyer present following his arrest had been violated. He also declared that Rifkin's confession was admissible as evidence despite the defense's attempts to have it suppressed.

Because of the insanity defense put forward, Judge Jones agreed that Rifkin could undergo further neurological testing before the trial started. He therefore set the date of jury selection for September 19, and the trial would take place in October.

To the surprise of everyone involved, Rifkin changed his plea just before the jury selection took place. He entered a plea of guilty to the murders of Lauren Marquez and Leah Evens. Judge Jones accepted the plea and sentenced Rifkin to 25 years to life for each murder.

The last trial took place two years after the first trial. During sentencing for the murder of Iris Sanchez, Rifkin finally stood before the court and apologized for the horrors he had committed.

Rifkin told the family members of his victims that were present in the court that he had never understood why he was driven to commit the murders. He said, "You all think I am nothing but a monster, and you are right. Part of me must be."

Carol DeLeon, sister of Iris Sanchez, described Rifkin to the court as a cold-blooded killer. She further said, "Iris was far from being perfect or an angel. But I will say that she did not have to die the way she did, strangled by the hands of Joel Rifkin, then dumped like garbage. Iris Sanchez will rest in peace in our hearts as of today, but you, Joel Rifkin, will now rot in hell."

Rifkin went on to say the following:

"I want you to know that I am sorry for what I have done to you and your daughters. I will go to my grave carrying the deaths of these innocent women with me. Some of you believe that I felt that their murder was in some way justified because they were prostitutes. But this is untrue. I never felt that way.

"Some of them were my friends and were kind to me. My victims were people with dreams and families, and some of them had children of their own.

"What I have done can never be forgiven, but I ask you to believe me when I tell you I will never understand the part of me that caused me to do those terrible things to your children.

"Not only will I go to my death reliving these horrors, but I will go there never knowing at all why I did committed them at all (sic).

"Please believe me that there are other Joel Rifkin's walking your streets right now. Like me, they will eventually be caught, but not until they have caused more suffering and deaths. I hope society can prevent this."(sic)

The presiding judge, Justice Robert Joseph Hanophy, said that it was unfortunate he was not able to sentence Rifkin to death. Because Iris Sanchez's murder had taken place before the capital punishment law had been re-enacted, a death sentence wasn't available.

In total, Rifkin was convicted of nine murders out of the seventeen and received 203 years imprisonment as a result. Although he may be eligible for parole at some point, it is highly unlikely he will ever be let out of prison. Because of the nature of his sentences, Rifkin has effectively been sentenced to serve out the remainder of his natural life behind bars.

CHAPTER 6:

SEARCHING FOR ANSWERS

Even though the families of the seventeen women Rifkin murdered now knew what had happened to their loved ones, and Rifkin had been tried and convicted for his crimes, many questions still remained, the most unsettling of which was the motive behind the murders. It was still unclear why Rifkin had become a killer, and even he himself had no idea.

An Interesting Brain

During one of his many interviews from prison, Rifkin was asked if he understood why he killed so many women. In response, he said the following:

"It was just something that happened and, you know, I had no plans to repeat it. Am I just evil? Am I brain-damaged? I mean, these are questions I want answered."

He wasn't the only one that wanted to know the answers. The families, law enforcement agencies, medical specialists, and scientific researchers also wanted to know. The general public wanted to know how Rifkin could have become such a monster, for fear there may be others out there just like him.

A research team from the University of Southern California, led by Monte Buchsbaum and Adrian Raine, decided to undertake a project that would use medical imaging of the brains of 25 murderers to see if there was a physiological reason for a person becoming a killer in the 1990s. One of those killers was Rifkin.

The results showed that many of the killers scanned had an abnormality in the frontal lobes of the brain. In normal brains, this area is the most active part of the brain, but in the scans of a murderer, they were a lot less active. This was an important discovery, because parts of the frontal lobes are believed to be involved in organizing and planning, which could explain why killers have such trouble with controlling their impulses.

Regarding the brain scans taken of Rifkin, psychiatrist Dr. Jonathan Pincus from Georgetown University said that the results were very much like the scans taken of other serious criminal offenders. Rifkin's frontal lobes were, in his words, "very, very, seriously damaged."

Despite the results, people don't become violent simply because of damage to their brain or a malfunctioning area of the brain. There are often a number of other factors, including mental disorders such as schizophrenia or a childhood affected by serious abuse.

A history of abuse can create underlying anger, of which the abused victim is waiting for it to be released. If this is combined with a deficiency of the functioning of the frontal lobe, then the combination of poor impulse control and the underlying anger becomes a volatile mix that is not easy to control.

Buchsbaum doesn't see this information as being the complete answer to the question of why some people kill. There is still much research to be done, and the last thing they want to do is create a scenario where violence can be excused as a result of this incomplete data.

It is not yet possible to determine if a person will become a killer based on their brain scans. They cannot predict how a person will be affected by their brain, their surroundings, or their upbringing for certain. However, the results do help to understand the issues of impulse control, and this may assist in developing methods and strategies to try and improve how a person manages their impulses.

Psychopathic Traits and Warning Signs

There are nine warning signs in childhood that can be interpreted to indicate the person is a psychopath. Following is a description of these signs and whether or not Rifkin showed these as a child.

1. Antisocial Behavior

A psychopath tends to be antisocial, not interacting with others outside of the home. They don't spend time playing with other children or seeking out contact.

- *Rifkin was a complete loner, with no friends and only one or two very brief and awkward relationships as a young man. He stayed at home the majority of his time, alone in his bedroom.*

2. Arson

When a child is lighting fires often, it is a sign that the child could grow up to be a serial killer. It is believed that they are drawn to arson because it enables them to exert some level of control and power over the flames.

- *There is no evidence that Rifkin carried out any form of arson as a child or an adult.*

3. Torturing Small Animals

This behavior is considered to be the most serious of all the warning signs, and children who enjoy torturing animals are more likely to become a sociopath and a serial killer. As children, they are able to exert control over the animal, just as the killer seeks to hold power over their human victims.

- *Rifkin liked animals, and there is nothing in his history to suggest he ever tried to torture or kill them.*

4. Poor Family Life

A large number of serial killers experienced an unstable childhood, where family members were involved in substance abuse, criminal activities, or suffered some form of mental illness. The relationship between the killer and their family is often complex and inefficient.

- *Although he was adopted, Rifkin lived in a loving home where he was treated very well. His mother was perhaps a little overprotective, but he enjoyed a good relationship with both of his parents and his sister.*

5. Childhood Abuse

There is a lot of evidence indicating that serial killers are often abused as children, either sexually, physically, or psychologically. This is generally considered relevant if the abuse is at the hands of a close family member, but there are numerous cases where the abuse was by a stranger or other member of the community.

- *He wasn't abused by a close family member, but Rifkin did suffer significant abuse at the hands of his peers, particularly while he attended school. He was constantly bullied, taunted, and at times, beaten by fellow students throughout his years at school.*

6. Substance Abuse

Many known serial killers had issues with abusing alcohol, drugs, or both.

- *It isn't clear what drugs Rifkin was taking at the time of committing the murders, but he did mention in his statements that he had indulged in drug use with his victims. There is no mention of him having trouble with alcohol.*

7. Voyeurism

Voyeurism is apparent in many serial killers from a young age.

This includes pornography, particularly that of a sadomasochistic nature, and fetishism.

- *Rifkin spent a lot of time in his bedroom watching pornography, but there is no evidence to suggest he would stalk or try and peep on women getting undressed. He was, however, obsessed with prostitutes, but this may have been more to do with his social isolation and lurid fantasies rather than actual voyeurism.*

8. Intelligence

Studies of many serial killers have shown that they tend to have a higher than average level of intelligence. Organized killers usually exhibit the higher range, whereas the disorganized tend to be at the lower end of the scale.

- *Although Rifkin struggled educationally and was dyslexic, his IQ was recorded as being fairly high, with a score of 128. He was also classified as an organized killer. By comparison, a genius level is generally considered to be any IQ over 140. One of the most intelligent serial killers is Ed Kemper, with an IQ of 136.*

9. Shiftlessness

Shiftlessness is common among serial killers, with many having menial or unskilled labor jobs, and they tend to have difficulty staying employed. Even though they are usually highly intelligent, they are unable to maintain a stable working life and often have jobs that are more physical than mental.

- *Rifkin was a landscaper and a gardener, and he lost several jobs because he just wouldn't turn up or he would leave before his duties were completed. Rifkin preferred to spend his time fantasizing about killing prostitutes rather than working. He only worked enough to raise the funds to pay for the working girls.*

Taking all of this into consideration, Rifkin doesn't meet all of the suggested criteria, but there are certainly areas where the warning signs were there. However, because he was never in trouble with the law and didn't seek any form of treatment for his social inadequacy or constant disturbing thoughts, he was completely under the radar, so nobody had a clue that these signs were there until it was far too late.

Classification and Method

The classification of serial killers based on their crime scenes according to whether they are considered organized or disorganized was the brainchild of a former FBI profiler, Ron Hazelwood. Along with other well-known agents, John Douglas and Robert Ressler, they conducted research on 36 known serial killers and looked at a variety of factors to reach their conclusions.

The factors analyzed include the following:

- Positioning or posing of the body

- Sexual acts before or after the death
- Cannibalism performed
- Mutilation or dismemberment of the body

The classifications of organized or disorganized are used as key differentials when profiling a serial killer.

Organized Killer

Rifkin is classified as an organized killer, even though it may not seem that he fits all of the aspects of the classification. Crimes committed by organized killers are carefully planned and premeditated, and there is often little evidence found at the crime scenes. These killers are often psychopathic and antisocial, but they still know right from wrong. They are not insane; they know what they are doing at the time of each murder. They also show no remorse for what they have done.

An organized killer is usually educated and of above average intellect, skilled, attractive, married or in a live-in relationship, employed, and usually controlling and cunning. Some of these killers are considered charming and often easily persuade their victims to go along with them. In these respects, it's difficult to see how Rifkin fits this category, but this can be further explained by the key components of each murder.

There are usually three separate crime scenes of an organized killer: the place where the victim is approached, where they are killed, and the disposal site. This is where Rifkin really fits the bill. All of his victims were picked up off the street, taken to either a motel or his house and killed, and then the bodies were disposed of in a variety of locations.

An organized killer is often difficult to capture because of the nature of their offenses. They go to extreme lengths to make sure they leave no clues or evidence behind, and they often have some degree of knowledge about police procedure and forensics. In Rifkin's case, he had been studying other serial killers, so he would have been aware of the mistakes they had made and how they were caught.

Method - Manual Strangulation

Killers use a variety of methods, but with serials, they tend to favor strangulation, especially if the victim is a female. There have been numerous serial killers who strangled their victims, and Rifkin is one of them. Some prefer to use a ligature rather than manual strangulation, but others prefer to feel their hands around the necks of their victims.

Strangulation causes death because it prevents blood from being supplied to the brain, leading to what is called cerebral hypoxia. The airways are shut off, so there is no oxygen going in or out of the body. In many cases, strangulation can result in unconsciousness in as little as 15 seconds, but it can take up to a few minutes for the victim to actually die.

There are a number of reasons why the victim of strangulation is predominantly female. This 'up close and personal' method of murder is more likely to be easier with a female because of their perceived inability to fight back. A male however, is generally much stronger so it is more difficult but not impossible, to kill by strangulation.

Females are often the victims also because they are the most common targets for sexual assaults, and the killer may use strangulation to overcome or prevent them from resisting during the act of rape. There have been cases where the killer will strangle his victim into unconsciousness then wait for them to waken before strangling them again. This heightens the feeling of power for the killer, and it can be repeated over and over with the victim until they finally succumb.

A study showed that ligature strangulation in sexual murders is associated with cruel and deliberate behavior at a crime scene. This is regarded as a predator murder pattern.

Some researchers have determined that the reason for strangulation as the chosen method in serial murders has to do with the positioning of the victim to the killer during the attack, particularly sexual attacks. Therefore strangulation is more convenient and easier to achieve. Of course, there is also the increased sense of power and control for the killer over their victim. For some, they experience great satisfaction staring at the eyes and face of their victim as they fight to live, and some killers have stated they got their biggest thrill watching the life drain out of their victim's eyes.

Dismemberment and Decomposition

For the majority of people, the thought of actually killing someone never enters the mind. But when a killer takes it one step further and dismembers the body of the victim, it is an act that is totally incomprehensible. The gore, the smell, the mess, let alone the physical act of taking a knife or saw to a fellow human being, is just sickening to the majority of people.

Dismemberment is often considered to be a form of sexual gratification, beyond sadism. Many psychologists believe it is a sexually driven act, though in many cases, it is also a way of disposing of a body in an easier manner. Serial killers like Rifkin cut up the bodies so they could disperse it to separate disposal sites rather than have the whole body in one place.

This isn't a new behavior by any stretch of the imagination, and it actually dates back to the era of the 1200s. Back then, torturing a person and cutting off their head was considered to be normal in society and, in some cases, an act that was celebrated. Decapitating a person was believed to be the most 'prestigious form of death'. In Korea during the 12th and 18th centuries, the 'four horse' method was often utilized. This involved tying the body to four horses and tearing it apart into five pieces.

Psychologically, when a killer is capable of dismembering their victim, it demonstrates their ability to disregard their victim as being of value, that their existence was unimportant. They are able to distance themselves from the victim, seeing the act of dismemberment as a means to an end rather than an abhorrent task.

When a killer dismembers their victim, they are in effect showing that they are aware of what they are doing. They know that cutting the body up helps with disposal, and they are aware that they are also doing so to gain a sense of ultimate domination over their victim. It often gives the killer an increased sense of their own self-worth, through the immense power they perceive to have elicited over their victim.

So, on one hand there are the killers who dismember to aid the disposal of the body and therefore help to prevent detection, and on the other hand, there are those killers who cut up their victims to achieve a higher level of sexual and personal gratification. Sometimes, these overlap, and the act of dismemberment is satisfying to the killer on all levels.

In Rifkin's case, it started out, he indicated in his statements, as a means to dispose of the body parts in various locations rather than trying to get rid of a body as a whole. But unlike many other killers, he found the act itself disgusting and incredibly messy, so he stopped doing it. Instead he found other ways to dispose of the bodies intact. However, the mess left behind in the garage of his home was not cleaned up appropriately, and when the home was searched, evidence of the dismemberments was clearly apparent.

When a Body Decomposes

Most of Rifkin's victims were disposed of fairly quickly after their deaths, except for the last one—the one he was caught with that ended his reign of terror over the local prostitutes. In that case, he had kept the body for at least three days, in the middle of summer no less, stored in his garage.

Between the heat and level of decomposition, it was no surprise that the foul odor of death was clearly recognized by the state troopers that pulled him over. The body in the back of his truck would have been putrid, and how Rifkin was able to tolerate handling the body in that state is beyond understanding. It is also remarkable that his mother and sister, who lived in the same house, didn't detect the smell.

There are four main stages of decomposition in humans and animals, and the science behind it all is a little grotesque, although highly useful when it comes to estimating time of death. Trained professionals, and even some law enforcement officers who have seen it too often, can determine when a person died by observing the state of their body.

Stage 1

This stage is called autolysis, which basically means 'self-digestion,' and occurs immediately after the person has died. When breathing stops and blood ceases to circulate, there is no way for the body to get rid of waste, and it is unable to absorb the oxygen necessary for keeping the cells alive.

This results in a build-up of carbon dioxide, and the body becomes acidic, leading to the rupture of membranes in the cells. These membranes then release certain enzymes which eat the cells from the inside.

Rigor mortis, the stiffening of the muscles, occurs during the first stage. The surface of the skin and the internal organs develop blisters, which are filled with nutrients. This gives the body a shiny look, and the top layer of skin starts to loosen away from the underlying structures.

Stage 2

This is the bloating phase. The enzymes that were leaked in stage one start producing high levels of gas. Bacteria that are already present in the body before death release compounds containing sulfur, and as these are released, the color of the skin changes. During bloating, the body can grow to twice its normal size.

It's during this stage that insects are drawn to the body. Bacteria and various microorganisms that are present create putrefaction, and this is where the decomposition smells come from. Often, it is the smell that alerts others to the presence of a dead body.

Stage 3

By now the skin, internal organs, and muscles have begun to

liquefy, and fluids are leaked through the body's orifices, such as the mouth and nose. It is during stage three that the majority of the body's mass is lost, leaving only bones, hair, and cartilage. This is known as the active decay stage.

Stage 4

The soft tissue, skin, and internal organs have decomposed now, and the remains have become skeletonized.

Timeline of Decomposition

The following timeline demonstrates how the time of death can be estimated based on the state of the human remains.

24 - 72 hours after death: decomposition of the internal organs.

3 - 5 days after death: bloating is present, and a foamy substance containing blood leaks from the nose and mouth.

8 - 10 days after death: the color of the body changes from green to red as the internal organs accumulate gas and the blood decomposes.

1 month after death: liquefaction of the body occurs.

Several weeks after death: teeth and nails fall out.

CHAPTER 7:

THE VICTIMS

Too often, it is easy to focus on the killer rather than the innocent people they killed. Sometimes this is because there just isn't a great deal of information about the victims due to the time elapsed or the family restricting what is released. But it is always important to remember that they are the ones who were lost, through no fault of their own, regardless of what their behavior or lives were like. Even though Rifkin's victims were all prostitutes with addictions, they were still human beings and just as important as any other victim out there.

First to Die, Last to be Identified

It took 24 years for Rifkin's first victim to be identified. He had recalled her name as being 'Susie', and when her head was found on the golf course in 1989, police had no idea who she was. She remained unidentified until March 2013, when newer techniques in identification were utilized to finally give her a name.

Authorities had accumulated a list of prostitutes who had been known to work in the areas of New York City where Rifkin found his victims. On that list, was a woman by the name of 'Susie Spencer', and given that Rifkin had called his first victim 'Susie', the name stood out for police.

A reconstruction of the head found on the golf course was compared to a mugshot taken of a drug addicted prostitute called Heidi Balch, who was known to use the name Susie Spencer. They were quickly matched by a cut that had been present above her right eye and a mole on her face.

Heidi's parents were then contacted and asked to submit DNA to determine one way or another if the remains did in fact belong to the missing woman. They were a match, and the family was finally given a sense of closure. They had always suspected she had met foul play but never knew for sure. Now they finally knew what had happened to their daughter and could lay her to rest.

A Family Disagrees

It can be hard on the families of victims to hear their loved ones painted in a rather unvirtuous light. They often have difficulty hearing that their daughter or sister was a drug addict or a prostitute, and sometimes they were simply unaware of what was going on in their lives at the time they disappeared.

For the family of Jenny Soto, they knew her as a completely different woman to the one she was portrayed as in the media and courtroom. For them, Jenny was a very nice girl, who had for a time dabbled in prostitution and drugs but had straightened herself out by the time of her murder.

They said Jenny had wanted to be a dancer or a model, and she liked to get dressed up and go out dancing in the clubs at night. She would spend hours grooming, making sure her hair was right before she went out. Her sister often went out with her, and they were out nearly every night. Jenny liked disco and rap music, and she had been planning on helping her brother's rap group with their production.

At home, Jenny was a lot quieter, but she hung out with what they considered to be a 'fast crowd' in Manhattan. She would dress in short miniskirts and wear large hoop earrings. Her mother refused to believe she had been a prostitute, despite seeing her police record, and assumed that because of the way she dressed they had mistaken her for a working girl.

When Jenny's body was found washed ashore on the Harlem River, she had been dressed in just a T-shirt. Her long fake fingernails were found to have skin beneath them, which indicated she had fought hard against Rifkin when he attacked her.

But it wasn't the first time this poor family had experienced murder. Jenny's father was murdered in 1968, stabbed to death in a subway station. It was no surprise that they felt Rifkin deserved to die for what he had done, taking away another loved one from this family.

Timeline of Their Deaths

March 5, 1989

The murder of 'Susie' later identified as Heidi Balch, 25. On this date, her remains—just her severed head—were found on a golf course.

It is unknown where her family has buried her remains.

1990 (Exact date unknown)

Julie Blackbird was picked up by Rifkin. After having sex, he struck her and killed her. He dismembered her body, set the parts in cement, and scattered the remains in the Hudson River.

Her body has never been found, but her family has a grave marked for her next to her grandparents at the Memorial Oaks Cemetery.

July 13, 1991

Picked up Barbara Jacobs, 31, and killed her when she fell asleep. Her body was disposed of in the Hudson River. It is unknown where her family has buried her remains.

September 1, 1991

Rifkin picked up Mary Ellen Deluca, 22. After sex, he asked her if she wanted to die and she said yes, so he strangled her. Her body was found at a rest stop in October.

September 23, 1991

The remains of Yun Lee, 31, were discovered after she had been disposed of in the East River. She was known to Rifkin, as they had met previously for sex. On this occasion, he was unable to perform, and he killed her on impulse.

December 26, 1991

Lorraine Orvieto, 28, was killed by Rifkin after he picked her up off the street for sex. She was put into an oil drum and dumped into the Coney Island Creek. It was discovered six months later.

January 2, 1992

Mary Ann Holloman, 39, was picked up by Rifkin as she walked along the street. She was strangled and put into an oil drum before being disposed of. Her family buried her at Saint Mary's Cemetery in Pittsburgh.

April, 1992 (Exact date unknown)

Rifkin picked up prostitute Iris Sanchez, 25. He strangled her during sex and left her body in a field near JFK International airport, hidden by an old mattress.

May 25, 1992

Anna Lopez, 33, was working as a prostitute when Rifkin picked her up. He paid her for sex and then strangled her to death. Her body was disposed of in woods located in Putnam County.

May - July, 1992 (Exact date unknown)

Rifkin picked up prostitute Violet O'Neill, 21, and took her back to the house for sex. He strangled her and dismembered the body before tossing her remains into the Hudson River area.

July, 1992 (Exact date unknown)
Unidentified 'Jane Doe', referred to as 'No Name #1', was murdered by Rifkin after he picked her up by the side of the road and had sex with her. Her remains were put into an oil drum and disposed of in the Newtown Creek.

1992 (Exact date unknown)
The second unidentified victim was picked up sometime between July and October. They had sex, and then Rifkin strangled her. Her body was placed in an oil drum and dropped into the Harlem River.

October 2, 1992
Another victim that Rifkin had known previously, Mary Catherine Williams, 31, had passed out in his car after he picked her up for sex. He tried to strangle her but was unsuccessful, so he smothered her instead.

November 16, 1992
The death of Jenny Soto, 23, was brutal. He picked her up for sex, and when he tried to strangle her, she fought back so violently that she broke every one of her fingernails, leaving marks on his face and neck. Eventually Rifkin broke her neck and then dumped her body over a cliff near the Harlem River.

February 27, 1993

Leah Evens, 28, was working as a prostitute to fund her drug habit when Rifkin picked her up. They had sex, and then he strangled her. She was the only victim who was buried, in a shallow grave on a farm in Northampton. It's unknown why she was buried and not disposed of like the others.

April 2, 1993

Rifkin picked up Lauren Marquez, 28, for sex, and almost as soon as the sexual act began, he strangled her. Her body was left in the Suffolk County Pine Barrens.

June 24, 1993

The final victim, Tiffany Bresciani, 22, was picked up and taken to a parking lot by Rifkin. He strangled her and then took her back to his house. Three days later, he was caught with her body while on his way to dispose of it.

CHAPTER 8:

MORE QUESTIONS THAN ANSWERS

Like with any serial killer case, there are often many more questions than answers. A number of notorious murderers have tried to provide answers, and in some cases seek those answers themselves, by granting interviews to anyone who will listen. Rifkin was one of those murderers. He wants to know for himself why he became a murderer and why he continued to kill.

Rifkin's Interviews

One of the most well-known interviews with Rifkin was conducted by FBI Profiler Mark Safarik. Although there is no transcript, the interview was recorded and can be watched online. Perhaps one of the most enlightening, yet surprising, revelations that came about during this interview was Rifkin's claims that he had formulated a plan to stop himself from killing.

Rifkin claimed he was due to talk to a realtor about a property in Virginia, far away from New York, but it never occurred because he was arrested before the meeting could take place. He said he was looking at 'doing a Unabomber'—referring to how the Unabomber, Ted Kaczynski, had isolated himself in a small cabin in the woods.

Rifkin's idea was that if he was alone in the woods with limited finances, he would be forced to spend what little money he would have on food and supplies instead of prostitutes. He believed that if he couldn't afford a prostitute, he wouldn't be in a position to kill them.

Anyone who has ever studied serial killers knows that this is nothing more than a bit of nonsense. It is well-known that they are incapable of stopping once they begin killing. That's why if a serial killer stops, the most likely reason is because they are either dead, disabled, or already in prison.

The obvious thing is that if Rifkin couldn't afford to pay for a prostitute, he would most likely have found victims another way. Safarik discussed with Rifkin the implausibility that his simple plan would have worked. But, that's what Rifkin believed.

Another interview Rifkin gave was to a television journalist from CBS2 named Mary Calvi, in January 2011. She began by talking to him about his murders before broaching the topic of the Long Island Serial Killer that was actively murdering women at the time.

Rifkin explained that he had told himself the prostitutes were nothing more than "drug addicted, disease-carrying vermin." Even though he knew it was a lie.

An interesting insight he provided when talking about how the Long Island Serial Killer's victims were discovered in groups of four, was how he himself had disposed of the bodies in groups of three.

"There were mini clusters, little sets of three," explained Rifkin. "Three were dismembered. Three were in oil drums. Some were in water. Some were on land. It's like my own little nightmare scenarios."

He admitted he had conducted research to help cover his tracks with each murder. He had looked at the past crimes of others to ascertain details that would enable him to continue without detection. He said during the interview, "Water is harder to investigate than land because it washes everything."

When asked if he would have killed again if he hadn't been caught, Rifkin answered, "As much as I say I wanted to stop, there probably would have been others."

Regarding his preference for selecting prostitutes for his victims, he said, "They're easy because they travel a lot. Then can disappear for months."

Calvi asked if he ever thought at the time about the lives of the women he murdered or their families. Rifkin responded, "You lie to yourself. You deny that there's a family. You deny that there's parents and possibly kids. You think of people as things."

Problems in Prison

Rifkin's life in prison hasn't exactly gone smoothly. Right from the beginning of his sentences, there was trouble. Early in 1994, he was involved in a 'scuffle' with Colin Ferguson, the Long Island Railroad mass murderer. Allegedly, the two men got into a fistfight over whose killings were better. Ferguson had been convicted of opening fire on commuters aboard a train, killing six.

Other stories surrounding the scuffle claim that it all started when Ferguson was trying to make a phone call and Rifkin wouldn't be quiet. Ferguson apparently said to Rifkin, "I wiped out six devils, and you only killed women." Rifkin responded, "Yeah, but I had more victims." It was at that point that Ferguson punched Rifkin in the face.

In 1996, Rifkin was transferred to Attica State Prison from Rikers Island. On arrival, he presented with a black eye, after having been assaulted while with fellow inmates. For Rifkin, prison was similar to the experiences he had at high school. He was constantly threatened or teased by the other inmates, so he was put into solitary confinement, where he would remain for four years.

Solitary confinement is the hardest time served both emotionally and physically. Inmates are kept in their cells, roughly the size of an average bathroom, for 23 hours a day. They experience no human interaction other than brief contact with prison officials when meals are presented or if there is a reason for a meeting. As well as lack of contact, prisoners in solitary confinement also have very little to do during the hours they are relegated to their cells, other than stare at the walls or perhaps undertake some drawing or writing. It is well established that long periods in solitary can severely impact the mental health of the inmate, leading to psychological damage.

Many of the inmates that are put into solitary confinement are in there because they are violent and a danger to others, including staff members. Rifkin, however, was put into solitary because of the effect his presence was having on other inmates, largely due to the infamy of his crimes. Four years seems like an excessive amount of time for Rifkin to have spent locked up in solitary confinement, but it is by no means the longest term prisoners have spent in that environment. Those with the longest times in solitary include:

Albert Woodfox

- 43 years in solitary

Woodfox was initially sentenced to 50 years for an armed robbery and was sent to the Louisiana State Penitentiary in 1971. In 1972, a correctional officer was murdered, and Woodfox, along with inmate Herman Wallace, were charged with the crime and sentenced to solitary confinement for 40 years. He was eventually released from prison in 2016, when he was 69 years old, after reaching a plea deal.

Herman Wallace

- 41 years in solitary

Wallace was also serving a sentence for armed robbery when he was charged along with Woodfox for the murder of the correctional officer and received the same sentence. In 2010, a documentary was made called the 'Land of the Free' which was based on the experiences of Woodfox, Wallace, and another inmate, Robert King, and the harsh conditions they endured in solitary confinement. Wallace was eventually released in 2013, but died three days later from cancer.

Tommy Silverstein

- 33 years in solitary

Silverstein had been convicted of multiple armed bank robberies and was sent to Marion Penitentiary in Illinois. He went on to murder four people while in prison, two inmates and two security guards. Sentenced to solitary confinement, the prison built a special unit for him, nicknamed the 'Silverstein Suite', and it is unexpected that he will ever be released back into the general population.

Ian Manuel

- 20 years in solitary

Manuel was only 13 years old when he was tried and convicted as an adult for shooting a woman in the face during a robbery.

Initially, he was put into solitary confinement for his own protection because of his age, but the isolation took a toll on his mental health, and he continuously acted out. To control his behavior, he was detained in solitary confinement. Eventually, he was released in 2016 with the help of his shooting victim, who fought for his release.

Robert Maudsley

- 39 years in solitary

Maudsley has spent the past 39 years locked in solitary confinement due to his murders of four people, including three fellow inmates. He currently holds the record for the longest time spent in solitary in a British prison. Maudsley spends 23 hours each day locked up in a bulletproof glass cell that was built for him in 1983, after he was designated as Britain's most dangerous prisoner.

Clinton Correctional Facility

Today, Rifkin resides within the confines of the Clinton Correctional Facility in Dannemora, New York. A maximum security state prison, it is often called 'Little Siberia' by inmates because of the bitterly cold climate of the area and its isolated location. It once housed the death row for New York and has a staff of approximately 1,000 prison guards.

There have been a number of well-known criminals contained at Clinton, including Rifkin, and the list includes inmates who were famous for their occupations as well as their crimes. A collection of murderers, rapists, thieves, and other immoral characters have all spent time under the same prison roof as Rifkin, although thankfully, not all at the same time.

Michael Alig

Alig was sentenced 10 to 20 years for murdering his drug dealer. Incarcerated in 1996, he was released on parole in May 2014.

David Berkowitz 'Son of Sam'

Serial killer Berkowitz extinguished the lives of six innocent victims and was sentenced to six life sentences with the possibility of parole after 25 years. To date, he is still incarcerated. He spent ten years in Clinton before being transferred to the Sullivan Correctional Facility.

Richard Bilello

Bilello was a member of the Lucchese crime family and was convicted of murder.

Robert Chambers

Also known as the 'Preppy Murderer', Chambers was convicted of killing Jennifer Levin and served most of his sentence at Clinton. He was later found to be in possession of heroin in his cell and faced charges related to that.

Gregory Corso

Corso, a poet of Italian-American descent, was sent to Clinton after being convicted of stealing a suit. He was a part of the inner circle of 'The Beat Generation.'

Jesse Friedman

Friedman was convicted of sexual abuse and sodomy of a child. He was featured in the documentary, 'Capturing the Friedmans.'

Robert F. Garrow

Garrow, a serial rapist and a murderer, served two sentences at Clinton. The first was for rape in 1961, and the second was for second-degree murder in 1974.

Paul Geidel

With the record of being the longest-serving prisoner in American history who was eventually released, Geidel was initially sent to prison for murder with a sentence of 20 years. However, he was found to be legally insane in 1926, and was moved to the Dannemora State Hospital. He later was returned to prison and granted parole in 1974, but by then he was 80 years old and did not want to leave. He had spent his entire adult life in prison and was fearful of coping on the outside. Eventually he was released in 1980, at the age of 86.

Maksim Gelman

Gelman went on a stabbing spree in 2011, which resulted in the deaths of four people and injuries to five others. He was sentenced to serve 200 years behind bars.

David Gilbert

A member of the Black Liberation Army, Gilbert was sent to prison for his participation in the attempted armed robbery of an armored car in 1981.

Timothy Ginocchetti

In 2006, Ginocchetti stabbed his mother to death, inflicting 30 knife wounds to her body. He was only sentenced to 15 years and spent time at Clinton until being transferred elsewhere.

Julio Gonzalez

In 1990, Gonzalez deliberately set a club called 'Happy Land' on fire, resulting in the deaths of 87 people. He was sentenced to a total of 4,350 years in prison.

John Jamelske

A mass kidnapper, Jamelske abducted and held five women for more than 15 years in a dungeon built in his house. In 2003, a sentence of 18 years to life was imposed upon him.

Vincent Johnson 'Brooklyn Strangler'

Johnson murdered five women between 1999 and 2000, and was sentenced to life imprisonment without parole.

John Katehis

Katehis is serving 25 years to life for the second-degree murder of George Weber, an ABC Radio personality.

Marlon Legere

In 2004, Legere shot and killed NYPD detectives Patrick Rafferty and Robert Parker when they attempted to stop him after his mother had called them for help with Legere. He was sentenced to life imprisonment without parole.

Charles 'Lucky' Luciano

One of the original crime bosses in America, Luciano was sentenced to 30 to 50 years for running a prostitution ring. He served a portion of his sentence before being deported back to Italy after the end of World War II.

Maino

Rapper Maino was sent to prison for a variety of crimes, including robbery and kidnapping.

Richard Matt

A convicted murderer, Matt and fellow inmate David Sweat

broke out of Clinton in 2015, and Matt was shot and killed by police while he was on the run.

Winston Moseley

Moseley was convicted of killing Catherine Genovese in 1964.

Carl Panzram

Serial killer Panzram confessed to killing 21 people, but not all of the murders could be proven. He was initially sentenced to 25 years to life, but he killed the laundry foreman while in prison and was subsequently sentenced to death. He was hanged on September 5, 1930.

Daniel Pelosi

Pelosi was convicted of murdering Ted Ammon, the wealthy husband of the woman Pelosi was having an affair with, in an effort to gain access to the money. He was also convicted of tampering with the jury, and ultimately sentenced to 25 years to life.

Ralph 'Bucky' Phillips

Phillips was sentenced to life imprisonment without the possibility of parole after shooting three New York State troopers to death in 2006.

Christopher Porco

In 2004, Porco killed his father with an axe and attempted to murder his mother in the same manner. He was sentenced to 50 years to life.

Altemio Sanchez 'The Bike Path Rapist'

Serial rapist and murderer Sanchez was convicted of killing three women and raping at least 14 others over a 25 year period.

Tupac Shukar

Legendary murdered rap star Shakur spent nine months in prison on a sexual abuse conviction in 1995.

Shyne - Moses Michael Leviy

Another rapper, Shyne was sentenced to 8 to 10 years for multiple convictions of weapons possession, assault, and reckless endangerment. On his release, he was deported back to Belize.

Eric Smith

When he was 13 years old, Smith sexually assaulted and murdered a four-year-old boy. He was sentenced to nine years to life.

Joel Steinberg

Steinberg was convicted of manslaughter and child abuse as a result of his *six*-year-old stepdaughter's death, as well as abuse of his common-law wife.

John Taylor

Taylor entered a Wendy's restaurant in Queens, New York City, on May 24, 2000, and opened fire. He shot seven employees, killing five and seriously wounding the other two. He was initially sentenced to death, but it was later changed to life without the possibility of parole.

Rifkin Today

Now in his early 50s, Rifkin will live out the rest of his life behind bars, whether he stays incarcerated at Clinton Correctional Facility or is at some point transferred to another facility. It is a long, lonely, and heavily restricted life he has to look forward to. Some may say he got off easy. But for him, perhaps the best he can hope for is an early death.

Appeals and Lawsuits

The family of Lorraine Orvieto filed a lawsuit against Rifkin for the wrongful death of Lorraine. In response, Rifkin supplied a handwritten brief regarding the character of Lorraine. He stated that because she was an AIDS carrier, she may have been "responsible for the eventual deaths of numerous individuals."

In November 1997, Rifkin attempted to sue the New York Daily News and prison officials, claiming they had wrongfully named him as being HIV-positive. He stated that this misinformation had led to him suffering from assaults by inmates, eventually resulting in him being moved to solitary confinement for his own safety.

Rifkin filed another lawsuit against the prison in 2000, claiming they had violated his constitutional rights by keeping him in solitary confinement. The court found that there were reasonable and appropriate grounds for keeping Rifkin in solitary, and they ruled in favor of the prison.

An appeal was lodged against Rifkin's convictions, and in December 2001, it was rejected. Although it was agreed that his confession in the murder of Tiffany Bresciani should have been excluded, the evidence of his guilt was overwhelming.

CHAPTER 9:
ADOPTED KILLERS

Rifkin wasn't the first criminal to use Adopted Child Syndrome as a defense in murder cases. It is seldom acknowledged as an actual disorder, but those who believe in its existence want it to be accepted by the criminal justice system and child psychologists. The question is whether or not adopted children are more likely to grow up and become murderers.

Adopted Child Syndrome

The important thing to acknowledge is that Adopted Child Syndrome is not believed to affect all adopted children. There is a small group that have been classed as having the disorder, and therapists like Dr. David Kirschner have been studying the prevalence of murders committed by adopted children for quite some time.

The basis of the syndrome is that children who are adopted are affected by a deep sense of abandonment and loss, even if they were just babies at the time. Children who were studied exhibited issues with anger, depression, and rejection, and it is believed that these factors may be enough to claim Adopted

Child Syndrome in defense of murders and other violent crimes.

Statistics have shown that as many as 16% of serial killers were adopted as children. They also indicated that these children were as many as 25 times more likely to murder their adoptive parents. It is easy to think 'wow, that's a high number', but when you look at it more closely, that is actually a small number of adopted children.

Every time a murder case mentions that a perpetrator was adopted, it creates an outcry from adoption services and the adoption community, as they believe it has a negative effect on the process of adoption. By stating the perpetrator was adopted, it creates a level of suspicion for all who were adopted. The adoption community is concerned that this may discourage people from adopting children.

Dr. Kirschner is often called to testify at trials where the defense of Adopted Child Syndrome is used in murder cases. There is another disorder that is sometimes used in the defense of an adopted person which is Reactive Attachment Disorder. This disorder was once considered to be controversial, but it is now recognized in the Diagnostic and Statistical Manual used by practitioners. This disorder is usually diagnosed in children who have been shifted from multiple homes or who had been institutionalized at some point.

The study of adopted children and the effects on their mental health has been around for a very long time. It is not a new issue and was documented by Dr. F. Clothier in 1943.

"Every adopted child at some point in his development has been deprived of this primitive relationship with his mother. This trauma and the severing of the individual from his racial antecedents lie at the core of what is peculiar to the psychology of the adopted child and is called upon to compensate for the wound left by the loss of the biological mother.

"Every child has recourse to phantasy (sic) when he finds himself frustrated, threatened, or incapable of dominating his environment. For the adopted child it is not a phantasy (sic) that these parents with whom he lives with are not his parents, it is reality.

"For the adopted child, the fantasy parents are obviously the unknown lost real parents. His normal ambivalence will make use of this reality situation to focus his love impulses on one set of parents and his hate impulses on another. He finds an easy escape from the frustrations inherent in his home education by assuming the attitude that these, his adoptive parents, are his bad and wicked persecutors, whereas his dimly remembered own or foster parents, from whom he was "stolen," are represented in his phantasy (sic) as the good parents to whom he owes his love and allegiance."

Child psychologist Dr. Marshall Schecter works with troubled children, and he believes that up to a third of cases are children who were adopted. His observations are similar to those of Dr.

F. Clothier, finding that many of the adoptive children showed symptoms of fantasy and wanted to act out against their birth parents, particularly the mother.

Dr. Marshall Schecter also found that there were often outbursts directed at the adoptive parents, with the children often saying, 'you're not my real parents.' It was relatively common for the male children to lie and steal, whereas the female children acted out seductively.

Suicide or attempted suicide is notable amongst adopted children, and a report in August 2001 by Slap, Goodman, and Huang stated that suicide or attempted suicide was more common among teenagers who had been adopted than those who were not. The report stated:

"The association persists after adjusting for depression and aggression and is not explained by impulsivity as measured by a self-reported tendency to make decisions quickly. Depression, impulsivity, and aggression during adolescence have been associated with both adoption and suicidal behavior. Studies of adopted adults suggest that impulsivity, even more than depression, may be an inherited factor that mediates suicidal behavior."

A study was undertaken by psychologist Margaret Keyes of the University of Minnesota in 2013. The study included 692 adopted children and 540 children who were not adopted, and lasted for three years. During that time, 56 of the children attempted suicide, and of those, 47 were adopted children.

In Summary

Although not all adopted children grow up to be murderers, there are enough statistics to suggest that the prevalence is relatively high. Is Adopted Child Syndrome a legitimate defense? That depends on the crime, the court, and ultimately, the jury. But there is certainly enough evidence for it to be studied further.

The reality is that while adoption is necessary to give children homes, there is initially a separation for the child from their birthparents, especially the mother. It is well established that neonates respond to sounds by their mother, both internal and vocal, while still in the uterus, so it doesn't matter whether the child is adopted at a later age or at birth, there is still a traumatic separation for the child.

Children who are adopted almost always begin to wonder at some stage about their birthparents. They have unanswered questions about who they were, where they come from, and why they were given up for adoption. For some adoptees, they eventually find their birthparents and get those answers. But for the majority, they never find out. This increases their feelings of loss, abandonment, anger, and depression. Ultimately, this has to have an effect on the behavior of the adopted child as they mature.

Cases of Adopted Children Who Killed Their Parents

Moses Kamin, 25

In 2012, Moses was charged with murdering his adoptive parents by strangulation. His mother was a medical professional and his father a psychologist.

Tucker Cipriano, 19

Tucker was convicted in 2012 for the murder of his adoptive father, and was sentenced to life without parole. His father was beaten to death with a baseball bat, and his adoptive mother and brother were also wounded.

Heather D'Aoust, 14

Heather was charged as an adult in 2008 for the murder of her adoptive mother. She struck her adoptive mother in the head with a blunt object, most likely a hammer. Heather had initially planned to kill everyone in the house and had a history of mental illness and emotional problems. She was sentenced to 16 years to life.

Aaron Howard, 19

In 2007, Aaron murdered his adoptive mother by bashing her in the head with a lead pipe. He was sentenced to life imprisonment.

Graham Beange, 20

Graham bludgeoned his adoptive father to death with a hammer and was charged in 2007. No conviction details are available.

Brandon Christopher Menard, 26

In 2006, Brandon was sentenced to three life sentences plus 25 years for multiple murders. He killed both of his adoptive parents and his teenage adopted sister.

Patrick Niiranen, 37

Patrick beat his adoptive parents to death with a hammer in 1997. He claimed he had been trying to find his birthparents but that his adoptive parents were preventing it. He also claimed he had suffered physical abuse and was using cocaine at the time of the murders.

Patrick Campbell, 39

In 1991, Patrick murdered his adoptive parents by bludgeoning them to death. He was given the death sentence.

Matthew Heikklia, 20

Matthew shot and killed his adoptive parents with a shotgun in 1991. He received a sentence of 60 years.

Larry Swartz, 17

In 1990, Larry stabbed both his adoptive parents to death. He was sentenced to life in prison.

Daniel Kasten, 19

Daniel killed his adoptive parents in 1987 by shooting them both in the head. He had originally intended to kill his adoptive siblings and grandparents but didn't go through with it.

Jeremy Bamber, 24

This case was slightly different, because the motive was money. In 1985, Jeremy killed his adoptive parents, his sister, and his two young nephews so he could claim a substantial inheritance.

Patrick DeGelleke, 14

Patrick killed his adoptive parents in 1984 by deliberately setting a fire. He was convicted and sent to prison, his sentence beginning in a juvenile facility because of his young age.

Other Adopted Killers

There are 22 serial killers known to date that were adopted as children. Rifkin is on the list of course, and the others are listed below.

Aileen Wuornos

Aileen and her brother were abandoned by their mother in

1960, just before Aileen turned four years old. They were adopted by their mother's parents, Lauri and Britta Wuornos. Their birthfather died in prison in 1969, after hanging himself.

Between 1989 and 1990, Aileen murdered seven innocent men while working as a prostitute, because she said they all tried to assault her. Her defense was self-defense, but she was sentenced to death and subsequently executed in 2002.

Ted Bundy

Ted was abandoned by his mother after his birth, and his grandparents raised him until he was three years old. His birth mother later married, and he was adopted by her husband, Johnny Culpepper Bundy when he was five.

Ted murdered at least 30 women between the years 1974 and 1978. He was sentenced to death and was subsequently executed in 1989.

Kenneth Bianchi

Kenneth was adopted by Nicholas and Frances Bianchi in 1951, when he was three months old. They raised him as an only child.

Kenneth, along with his cousin Angelo Buono, became the Hillside Strangler duo, and was charged with the murders of twelve women. Kenneth entered an insanity plea, but it was rejected, and he was sentenced to life imprisonment.

Richard Speck

Although Richard was raised by his birthmother, she remarried a man after his father's death, and Richard and his numerous siblings suffered greatly at the hands of their stepfather.

In 1966, Speck killed eight student nurses after raping and torturing them in their townhouse. One of the women managed to survive by hiding. He was initially sentenced to death but it was overturned, and he died in prison of heart failure in 1991.

Albert DeSalvo

Forever known as the Boston Strangler, Albert was raised by his birthparents, so he wasn't actually adopted but was brought up in an extremely violent household. By the time he was 12, he was sent to live in a boy's reform school, so in essence, he experienced the same isolation and abandonment as those who were adopted.

Although he claimed to have murdered 13 women, Albert was never charged with murder. He was however, sent to prison for a number of rapes he had committed. He was murdered while in prison.

Tommy Lynn Sells

When Tommy and his twin sister Tammy were just 18 months old, they contracted meningitis. Tammy died, and not long afterwards, Tommy was sent to live with his aunt. He stayed with her until he was five, before going back to his mother. When he was eight, his mother gave a man she knew consent to abuse Tommy.

Although Tommy claimed to have committed 70 murders, authorities think the number is closer to 21. He was charged with just one murder and sentenced to death. He was executed in 2014.

Max Gufler

Little information is available about the childhood of Max, but he was convicted of killing four women he had lured using personal ads. It's believed he killed 18 or more women, and he was sentenced to life in prison in 1961. A few years later, he died.

Christian Longo

When Christian was three years old, his parents got divorced, and his mother subsequently remarried. Her new husband, Joseph Longo, adopted Christian. He grew up in what he called a happy home, and they were heavily engaged with the Jehovah's Witness church.

In 2001, Christian murdered his wife and three young children and then fled to Mexico. He was later caught in 2002, and after he was convicted, he was sentenced to death.

Joseph Kallinger

Joseph was born to parents Joseph and Judith, and in 1937, his father left the family and Joseph was placed into foster care. In October 1939, he was adopted by Austrian couple Stephen and Anna Kallinger. Joseph later claimed he was severely abused by his adoptive parents, including being whipped and starved. He was made to eat feces, burned, and locked in closets. When he was nine, he was sexually assaulted by boys in the neighborhood.

Between 1974 and 1975, Kallinger and one of his sons went on a crime spree which resulted in the murders of three people including one of his other sons. He received a life sentence and died of heart failure in 1996.

Lawrence Bittaker

Lawrence was born in 1940 to a couple who had never wanted children in the first place. He was put into an orphanage, and while still an infant was adopted by George Bittaker and his wife.

Along with Roy Norris, Lawrence later embarked on a killing spree that would leave the two men known as 'The Toolbox Killers.' Together, they murdered five teenage girls. Lawrence received the death sentence.

Charles Albright

Charles was born in Amarillo, Texas, and placed into an orphanage straight away. He was adopted by Fred and Delle

Albright while still a baby. His adoptive mother was strict and seemed overprotective, and encouraged any hobbies or interests he developed.

Charles later became known as the Eyeball Killer, after he murdered three women in 1991 and removed their eyeballs. He was sentenced to life imprisonment.

Jane Toppan

Born Honora Kelley in 1857, her parents Bridget and Peter were immigrants from Ireland. When she was young, her mother died from tuberculosis. Her father was known as an abusive alcoholic, and a few years after their mother died, Honora (Jane) and her sister Delia, were taken to the Boston Female Asylum, an orphanage. Honora (Jane) was just six years old at the time.

Honora (Jane) was eventually placed in the home of Ann Toppan to work as an indentured servant. Although she was never formally adopted, she took on the surname of the household and her name eventually changed to Jane.

While working as a nurse in 1901, Jane murdered at least 31 people. She was found not guilty by reason of insanity.

Thomas Hamilton

Thomas was born on May 10, 1952, to parents Thomas Sr. and Agnes. Not long after he was born, his parents separated and later divorced. Thomas and his mother went to live with his grandparents, who adopted him in 1956. For most of his life, he thought his mother was his sister.

On March 13, 1996, Thomas entered Dunblane Primary School with an arsenal of guns and opened fire. He killed 17, including one adult and 16 children, before killing himself.

Steven Catlin

Born in 1944, Steven was adopted by Glenn and Martha Catlin as an infant and lived in Bakersfield up until the early 1950s. By the time he was 19 years old, he was already in trouble with the law and spent nine months in a Youth Authority Camp for forgery.

Between 1976 and 1984, Steven killed two of his wives and his adoptive mother so that he could collect their insurance money. In 1990, he was sentenced to death.

Eric Payne

When Eric was just four months old, his father killed his mother and then committed suicide by hanging. At the age of eight, Eric was adopted by Gerald Payne, but by the time he was 14, Gerald had to surrender him back into the care system. Eric spent the next 18 years living in 22 foster homes, shelters, and institutions.

In 1997, Eric raped and killed two women. He used a hammer to beat them to death. He received the death sentence and was executed in 1999.

Gerald Stano

At birth he was named Paul Zeininger but was severely neglected by his birthmother until she surrendered him to an orphanage when he was six months old. By then, he was in such a terrible physical and emotional state that the doctors assessing him believed him to be unsuitable for adoption. His level of functioning was so poor that to survive he would eat his own feces. However, a nurse by the name of Norma Stano did adopt him and renamed him Gerald Stano.

Gerald murdered 22 women between 1969 and 1980, but in his confession, he claimed the figure was actually higher than 40. He was sentenced to death and executed in 1998.

Jurgen Bartsch

Jurgen was an illegitimate child born in Germany, and when he was five months old, his mother died of tuberculosis. For the next six months, he was looked after by nurses, and then he was adopted by a butcher and his wife. His adoptive mother suffered from obsessive compulsive disorder and was so focused on cleanliness that Jurgen was restricted from interacting with other children. She bathed him until he was 19.

Between 1962 and 1966, Jurgen murdered four young boys. He was sentenced to life in prison but died accidentally in 1979 after a nurse administered too much of the drug Halothane.

Alton Coleman

Alton's mother worked multiple jobs to support the family, so Alton was sent to live with his grandmother. He was bullied and teased for constantly wetting his pants as a child, and by the time he was in his teens, he was getting into trouble with the law.

In the space of a month in 1984, Alton, along with his girlfriend Debra Brown, went on a spree that resulted in seven murders. He received the death sentence and was executed in 2002.

Robert Otis Coulson

Robert and his sister Robin were abandoned by their mother when Robert was four years old and Robin was five. Their parents had separated, and their mother's new boyfriend didn't want any kids. Their natural father signed away his rights, and the two children ended up being cared for by child welfare workers. They were adopted by Otis and Mary Coulson, who already had another adopted child, Sarah.

In 1992, Robert killed his parents, both sisters, and his brother-in-law by subduing them, tying them up, and suffocating them using plastic bags over their heads. He then set the bodies and the house on fire. He was sentenced to death and was executed in 2002.

David Berkowitz

David was born 'Richard David Falco' on June 1, 1953, in Brooklyn. His mother gave him up for adoption just a few days after his birth, and although the reason for it is not certain, it's believed that because she had gotten pregnant by a married man, he forced her to give up the baby. David was adopted by Nathan and Pearl Berkowitz as an infant and renamed as David Richard Berkowitz.

Between July 1976 and July 1977, David murdered six people and wounded a further eight. He was convicted and sentenced to serve six life sentences.

James Munro

James was adopted at a slightly later age, when he was one year old. As an adult, he became an accomplice to William Bonin, the 'Freeway Killer', and was involved with approximately 44 murders. However, he was only ever tried and convicted for the murder of Steven Jay Wells and received a sentence of twenty years. His parole has been consistently denied.

Fact or Fiction?

So, although it seems there may be some credence given to the possibility of an Adopted Child Syndrome, it is yet to be considered a 'real' mental illness. When studying serial killers, researchers are constantly looking for similarities or factors that may give an indication into why people become murderers.

It is no surprise then that these similarities among adopted children who then become killers have been focused on by a number of esteemed psychologists. After all, in the cases mentioned above, all were either adopted or separated from their birth families, most at a very young age.

There is no doubt that the driving force behind many troubled youths and adults that suffer some sort of mental illness is often a sense of abandonment or isolation. Even if they end up in a happy and well-functioning family home, they still feel a sense of being 'different.' But is it really enough to say that Adopted Child Syndrome should be considered a legitimate defense in murder trials?

At no time before or after his arrest and trials did Rifkin ever put any sort of blame on his birthparents or his adoptive parents. By all accounts, his adopted family life had no dysfunctions or major issues. He wasn't abused by his adoptive parents and sister. He didn't grow up in a home filled with alcohol and drugs. Rifkin had a normal upbringing by his adoptive parents.

Many of the other cases of adopted children who become killers didn't have the same experiences as Rifkin. Some, such as Aileen Wuornos, ended up in an even more dysfunctional family unit, even though they were directly related by blood. In her case, she suffered more abuse at the hands of her grandparents who had taken on the responsibility of raising her.

It begs the question of whether it is the separation from the birthparents that causes the most problems for the adopted child mentally or the nature of the home environment they are adopted into. The focus of the reasoning behind Adopted Child Syndrome has largely concentrated on the separation rather than the homes they ended up in.

There may well be cases where there is clear evidence that the killer suffered from Adopted Child Syndrome and it should be considered as a legitimate defense at trial. But in Rifkin's case, it is not really surprising that his attempt to use it in his defense failed. He wasn't a troubled child, his adoptive home was settled and safe, and he didn't display the symptoms in childhood that are usually considered indicators for Adopted Child Syndrome.

Instead, the most likely contributing factor in shaping the mind of Rifkin was the excessive bullying and torment he suffered at the hands of his peers. That alone drove him into an isolated world, one where he spent all of his time on his own, typically in his bedroom as a child. There, he had all the time in the world to let his imagination run riot without the interference or opinions of others.

Basically, Rifkin retreated into his own world, and by doing so, he lost the ability to develop normal relationships with other people. The only ones who didn't judge him were the prostitutes. As long as he paid them, they didn't care who he was or what he looked like. They weren't meeting up for conversation, after all.

It is somewhat unfortunate that there is no acknowledged defense of killing because of the bullying and abuse experienced at school or as a young teen. It is possible to use abuse by parents or partners, but nothing exists for those who were tormented on a regular basis by fellow children. Yet, it is this abuse that appears to have a much larger effect on the development of a child's mind. It affects their confidence, self-esteem, and their ability to trust others.

A common denominator in many serial killers is abuse as a child. For that reason, the abuse suffered on the playground or by other children should be just as important as that meted out by a parent, sibling, or other such relative. The long-term effects on the psychological development are just as real and long-lasting.

It is very important to note though, that not all abused children grow up to kill, just as all children 'diagnosed' with Adopted Child Syndrome don't eventually become killers. In reality, it is a very small percentage in both cases. The number of abused children throughout the world is enormous, tragically, but the percentage of those that become serial killers is minute in comparison.

Likewise, if the figures are correct, if there are 16% of adopted children becoming killers, there are still 84% who don't. And there are a very large number of children adopted around the world. So, although 16% may seem to be high, there are a lot of other contributing factors that may be relevant as well.

In summary, the question of whether or not Adopted Child Syndrome should be a legitimate defense is a complicated one. There is definitely evidence that it exists. But can the blame really just be put on that diagnosis? Should a person walk free from a multiple murder trial because of it? After all, they still know right from wrong, and they knew what they were doing—it is not an insanity defense.

Adopted Child Syndrome may be a contributing factor, but it doesn't seem plausible that it should be the reason for a serial killer being exonerated of all responsibility. Rifkin, for example, knew exactly what he was doing. He fantasized about it for most of his youth and planned it all out. He made a conscious decision to kill all those women. He may not understand why, and he may well have suffered from Adopted Child Syndrome, but he could have stopped himself.

CHAPTER 10:

LONG ISLAND SERIAL KILLER?

An unidentified serial killer is believed to be responsible for at least ten murders, maybe as many as sixteen, in the Long Island towns of Oak Beach, Gilgo Beach and Jones Beach State Park. The victims were known to be associated with prostitution, and authorities think the murders took place over a period of twenty years. This killer became known as the Long Island Serial Killer, the Gilgo Beach Killer, and the Craigslist Ripper. Because of the similarities between the murders and those committed by Rifkin, as well as the location, Rifkin was considered a possible suspect.

Background of the Case

The first body was found in December 2010, while a police officer and his dog were engaging in a training exercise. The body had completely decomposed, with just skeletal remains left. The body was found encased in a burlap sack, which had also rotted away and almost disintegrated.

Two days later, police found three more bodies in the same area, the north side of the Ocean Parkway in Suffolk County. The local Police Commissioner was quick to agree that it was most likely the work of a serial killer, considering so many bodies were found in the same location and in a similar condition.

Four more bodies were discovered at the end of March 2011, and beginning of April. These bodies were in a different area off the parkway, but in close proximity to each other. The authorities decided to broaden their search area to include the border of Nassau County.

Around April 11, police began searching for more victims in Nassau County, and by now the New York State Police were also involved in the investigation. This search resulted in the discovery of partial human remains and the skull of yet another victim, bringing the total to ten victims since the prior December.

Two teeth were found near the skull on April 22, and then on June 16, the police had raised the reward offered from $5,000 to $25,000, for any information that would lead to the arrest of the Long Island Serial Killer.

Composite sketches were made of two of the victims that couldn't be identified, and these were released to the media on September 20, 2011. One of the victims found in April had been a toddler, and the police also released information about the jewelry found with the toddler and what was presumed to be the body of her mother that was found with her.

A further development was that one of the set of remains that had been found on April 11 matched a previous case where a garbage bag containing two human legs had washed ashore in 1996 on Fire Island. This gave a good indication as to how long the victim had been dead for. By September 22, 2011, police had received an astonishing number of tips, but none of them panned out.

It wasn't until November 29, 2011, that the authorities finally informed the public that the deaths of the ten victims were the work of one serial killer. They also believed that killer was living in Long Island.

The discovery of the remains of Shannan Gilbert on December 13, 2011, brought with it an enduring controversy, leading to speculation that her death was in fact a murder, rather than the accidental death it was initially considered to be. Her body was found in a marsh, and police thought she had drowned accidentally after falling in the marsh. However, the last known sighting of Shannan was of her banging on the door of a nearby residence screaming for help. The homeowner refused to let her in, and she ran off. Emergency services also received a call from Shannan that night during which she said "they were going to kill her."

Shannan's family firmly believed she was a victim of the Long Island Serial Killer, and they battled continuously to get the authorities to treat her death as a murder rather than a terrible accident.

Just before the five year anniversary of the discovery of the first victim, the Suffolk County Police Department made the announcement that the FBI was now assisting with the investigation. They had already helped with the search for bodies, but until this date, December 10, 2015, they hadn't officially been involved.

Victims

Some of the victims have been identified, but there are still many who have not. It is believed that there are still bodies out there, waiting to be found, and the investigation is ongoing.

Maureen Brainard-Barnes, 25

Maureen was an escort from Norwich, Connecticut, who advertised herself online. She was a tiny woman, standing just four feet eleven inches, and she only weighed 105 lbs. A single mother, Maureen placed ads on Craigslist offering her services as an escort to pay her mortgage and feed her family.

On July 9, 2007, Maureen traveled to New York City just to spend the day there and was never seen again. Her remains were discovered in December 2010.

Melissa Barthelemy, 24

Like Maureen, Melissa had also been advertising her services as an escort on Craigslist. She was last seen alive on July 10, 2009. That night, she had met with a client and $900 was deposited into her bank account. She tried to call an ex-boyfriend, but was unable to get through. For several weeks after her disappearance, her sister, who was just a teenager at the time, received a number of disgusting calls from Melissa's cellphone. The caller would ask if she 'was a whore like her sister', and eventually, after five weeks of calling, the caller said that Melissa was dead and he would 'watch her rot'.

Although police were able to trace some of the calls, they were unable to catch or identify the person responsible. Melissa's remains were discovered in December, 2010.

Megan Waterman, 22

Originally from South Portland, Maine, Megan disappeared after advertising on Craigslist as an escort, on June 6, 2010. She had told her boyfriend the day before that she would call him later, but never did. She was staying at a motel, not far from Gilgo Beach when she disappeared. Megan's body was discovered in December, 2010.

Amber Lynn Costello, 27

Amber lived in a town just ten miles away from Gilgo Beach. She was a user of heroin, and advertised herself as a prostitute on Craigslist. On the evening of September 2, 2010, Amber agreed to meet a client who had offered her $1,500 for her services, and she was never heard from again. Her body was also found in December, 2010. Her sister, who works as a call girl, used the same system of advertising on Craigslist in an effort to act as 'bait' for the killer.

Jessica Taylor, 20

Jessica had worked as a prostitute in both Manhattan and Washington D.C., before she disappeared in July 2003. Unlike the other victims who were buried in burlap sacks, her remains were found in pieces, the first of which were discovered the same month she disappeared. Her torso was found in Manorville, New York, 45 miles east of Gilgo Beach. The torso was lying on plastic sheeting, on a pile of wood at the end of an access road, and a tattoo had been mutilated, most likely to prevent identification.

In March, 2011, the hands, forearm and part of a skull were found at Gilgo Beach, and these were later identified as belonging to Jessica.

Jane Doe No. 6

Body parts including a head, hands and one foot, were found on April 4, 2011, and were determined to belong to the same woman whose remains were found on November 19, 2000, in Manorville - the same area as Jessica's remains. The torso of the unidentified woman was found in garbage bags in a wooded area near an intersection at Halsey Manor and Mill Roads. Although police have not been able to identify Jane Doe No.6, they were able to create a composite sketch. They believe this victim most likely worked as a prostitute, was somewhere between the ages of 18 and 35, and stood five feet two inches in height.

John Doe

Unusually, one of the victims was a male, and the body was discovered on April 4, 2011, in Gilgo Beach. An Asian male, this victim had died from what appeared to be blunt-force trauma. A composite sketch was created and released to the media in September, 2011. Police believed the victim had been dressed in women's clothing and most likely worked as a prostitute. The age of the victim was estimated to be between 17 and 23, and he had been around five feet six inches tall. Four of his teeth were missing, and it was estimated he had been dead for up to ten years.

Baby Doe

On April 4, 2011, the remains of a baby were discovered approximately 250 feet from the remains of Jane Doe No. 6. The baby was estimated to be between 16 and 24 months old. The remains were wrapped in a blanket, and there were no apparent injuries present. Originally it was thought that the baby had belonged to Jane Doe No. 6, but DNA testing showed her to be the infant daughter of Jane Doe No. 3, who was discovered 10 miles away.

Jane Doe No. 3 'Peaches'

This victim was initially nicknamed 'Peaches' because of a detailed tattoo that was present on the breast depicting a peach shaped like a heart with a bite out of it. The torso was found on June 28, 1997, in a Rubbermaid container by the side of a road to the west of Hempstead Lake in Lakeview. Further human remains were found in a plastic bag near Jones Beach State Park on April 11, 2011, and police dubbed this victim Jane Doe No. 3. In December 2016, both sets of remains were identified as belonging to the same person, an African-American female.

Jane Doe No.7

At Torbay Beach, near Gilgo, a skull and some teeth were found on April 11, 2011. Using DNA testing, these remains were identified as being linked to the legs found on Fire Island on April 20, 1996.

Other Potential Victims

Although these victims have not been formally linked to the Long Island Serial Killer, they remain as potential victims and police are actively reviewing their cases.

Tina Foglia, 19

Tina was last seen at a music venue in West Islip in the early hours of the morning on February 1, 1982. A known hitchhiker, her dismembered body was found February 3, on the shoulder of the Southern State Parkway. Her body parts had been placed into three garbage bags. Along with a missing piece of jewelry, DNA was found on the bags belonging to an unknown male.

'Cherries'

An unidentified female, she was nicknamed 'Cherries' due to a tattoo of two cherries on her breast. Her dismembered torso was found in a suitcase on March 3, 2007, which had washed ashore at Harbor Island Park, Mamaroneck. Medical examiners determined she had been stabbed to death. On March 21, one of her legs washed in with the tide at Cold Spring Harbor, and the other leg was discovered the next day at Oyster Bay. Because of the method of dismemberment and disposal, her murder may be linked to those of Jessica Taylor, Jane Doe No. 3, and Jane Doe No. 6.

Tanya Rush, 39

A similar case, the dismembered remains of Tanya Rush were found in a suitcase in June 2008, along the shoulder of the Southern State Parkway. Tanya was from Brooklyn, had three children, and was believed to be a prostitute.

Shannan Maria Gilbert

As mentioned previously, there has been a lot of speculation regarding the death of Shannan. With police and the original medical examiner stating her death was due to misadventure, or inconclusive, Shannan's mother refused to accept it given the circumstances on the night she disappeared.

In September 2014, Dr. Michael Baden was asked to redo an independent autopsy on the remains of Shannan to see if a definite answer could be obtained as to the manner of her death. He discovered the hyoid bone in her neck had been damaged, an indicator that she may have been strangled. Also, he found it was uncommon for someone who had drowned to be found face up, as Shannan was.

Despite the findings and opinion of Dr. Baden, Shannan's death is still listed officially as an accident. Her mother continued to fight, including suing the police, but tragically she herself was murdered by her other daughter who suffered from a mental illness on July 23, 2016.

Unidentified

The remains of an unidentified woman were found on January 23, 2013, by a lady out walking her dog. The body had been buried in brush along the shore of Sheep Lane near Oyster Bay. She was believed to have been Asian, and was wearing a gold pig pendant, which suggested it was a reference to the Chinese 'Year of the Pig', indicating she may have been 29 years old at the time of her death. Authorities think she was buried sometime before the area was hit by Hurricane Sandy in late 2012.

Natasha Jugo, 31

Natasha was last seen on March 16, 2013, as she left her home in Queens. Her vehicle was found along Ocean Parkway, and some of her clothing and personal items were discovered at Gilgo Beach. Her body washed ashore at Gilgo Beach on June 24, 2013. Police are not certain that Natasha was a murder victim, partly because she had a history of some sort of paranoia, often thinking someone was following her.

Rifkin Considered a Suspect

With nothing being found at the crime scenes to point toward a specific suspect, a profile was created with the assistance of the FBI to help the authorities try and identify who could possibly be responsible for the murders. One serial killer who seemed to fit the profile was Rifkin.

Investigators believed the killer was most likely white, aged between the mid-20s to mid-40s, and was either a local of the area or very familiar with it. He also had an occupation where he had access to burlap sacks, as these were used to dispose of the bodies. They believed the killer had a good understanding of law enforcement techniques, and may have even been a police officer or had close ties to the force.

The profile also indicated the killer would be married or in a steady relationship and be well educated. He was most likely financially secure and probably owned an expensive vehicle, maybe a truck. The killer was most likely employed as well. There was some suggestion that the killer could have sought medical treatment for 'poison ivy', as it was present at the dumping sites.

There had been two serial killers in Long Island that were known and apprehended, one being Rifkin and the other Robert Schulman, and both men were considered-potential suspects in the Gilgo Beach murders. Rifkin was quickly ruled out however, as he was already in prison at the time the murders were believed to have taken place.

Schulman had been a postal worker on Long Island, and was responsible for the murders of five prostitutes between 1991 and 1996. He was sentenced to death for one of the murders, because New York had reinstated the death penalty, and received life sentences for the other murders. He died while incarcerated. But, although his pattern and methodology seemed to fit the profile of the Gilgo Beach murderer, he was also ruled out because like Rifkin, he had scattered the bodies of his victims rather than bury them in specific areas.

Suspects

John Bittrolff

Considered to be very high on the list of suspects, Bittrolff was convicted for the murders of two prostitutes in 1993 and 1994. He is also suspected of being responsible for a third murder from that same period of time.

Robert Biancavilla, prosecutor for the Suffolk County District Attorney, released a statement on September 12, 2017, stating that Bittrolff was most likely responsible for other murders of women. He also said, "There are remains of the victims at Gilgo that may be attributed to the handiwork of Mr. Bittrolff, and that investigation is continuing."

There were a number of similarities between some of the Gilgo Beach murders and those Bittrolff had been convicted of. He lived in Manorville, where he worked as a carpenter, and this is where the dismembered torsos of Jane Doe No.6 and Jessica Taylor were found. The location of the bodies was just three miles away from Bittrolff's house. Bittrolff was a hunter who enjoyed mutilating and killing animals, and claimed to have once eaten the raw heart of a deer he had killed.

An important link between Bittrolff and the Gilgo Beach murders was that the daughter of one of his victims had been friends with Melissa Barthelemy, a victim of the Long Island Serial Killer. According to Melissa's mother, her daughter had received a lot of phone calls from the Manorville area before she disappeared.

James Burke

Burke was the former Police Chief in Suffolk County, and he was brought to attention as a potential suspect in response to claims made by the family of Shannan Gilbert. In December 2016, the family claimed through their attorney that Burke was rumored to have engaged in sexual activity with prostitutes, and that one of the women had claimed he had rough sex with her and choked her during a party at Oak Beach.

It was also discovered that while he was police chief, Burke had deliberately blocked the FBI from probing the Long Island Serial Killer murders. In November 2016, Burke faced charges of conspiracy to obstruct justice and a civil rights violation, after seriously assaulting a man who stole a bag filled with pornography and sex toys from Burke's vehicle. He was sentenced to 46 months in federal prison.

Joseph Brewer

Brewer, who lived in Oak Beach, was one of the last-known people to have seen Shannan Gilbert alive. He had hired her the night she disappeared for her services as an escort, after seeing her advertisement on Craigslist. He claims that not long after she arrived at his home, she started acting in an erratic manner, and then she took off, leaving his home. It was in the same neighborhood that Shannan was seen running and beating on doors begging for help. Police eventually cleared him as a suspect.

James Bissett

Bissett was a local businessman, who owned an aquarium, and just two days after the body of Shannan Gilbert was found, he committed suicide. This raised suspicion that perhaps he had been involved in the murders, and rumors were rife in the neighborhood. Suspicions increased when it was discovered Bissett also owned another business, a nursery, and therefore had access to burlap sacks. Despite all of this, police deny he was ever considered a suspect.

Dr. Peter Hackett

Hackett also lived in Oak Beach, and was actually a neighbor of James Brewer. Shannan Gilbert's mother received a phone call from Hackett two days after Shannan disappeared, and he told her he was looking after Shannan at his home for wayward girls. He called her again, five days later, but he later denied ever making contact with her. But, phone records proved that he did make the calls. His backyard was also very close to the marshy swamp where Shannan's remains were eventually found.

Investigations later found that Hackett had a habit of inserting himself into major events, and at times exaggerated his roles in such events. They also found that on the night Shannan disappeared, Hackett's wife and children were at home, so if anything had taken place, they would have been aware of it. He was eventually ruled out as a suspect.

Rifkin Talks About the Long Island Serial Killer

In an interview with the Daily News in 2010, Rifkin said that he wasn't impressed by the Long Island Serial Killer's methods, particularly the way he had disposed of the bodies in one area. By dumping all the bodies in the same place, Rifkin said that it brought more 'heat' to the case because it was more readily apparent to police that there was a serial killer at work.

According to Rifkin, he was always more concerned about disposing of his victims than he was about the actual acts of murder and dismemberment. He said, "I was surprised I didn't get caught sooner."

Rifkin suggested police should focus their investigation on white men aged between 18 and 45. But, acknowledging how massive a task that would be, he said, "That's like half the country."

He said the killer probably grew up in a similar manner to himself, with bullying and loneliness, and most likely suffered from anger. He stated, "America breeds serial killers. You don't see any from Europe."

In another interview, Rifkin said he had been following the Long Island Serial Killer case through news reports on television, and he had come up with his own theory, particularly regarding the four known prostitutes that were the first victims found.

He suggested the killer would be someone for whom the use of burlap sacks was a normal thing, so would go unnoticed. He pointed to jobs such as clam fisherman, landscapers, or contractors. Rifkin also suggested that the four bodies found on Gilgo Beach in December could have been totally unrelated to those discovered in Nassau and Suffolk counties.

The authorities working on the case say that Rifkin's thoughts on the case are those of someone who doesn't have the education in criminal investigation required to develop any sort of profile of a killer. Just because Rifkin is a serial killer it doesn't mean he knows how other serial killers think.

During the interviews, Rifkin was asked why prostitutes are often the main targets of serial killers. He explained that in his opinion it was because they had no family and could easily be missing for months before anyone noticed. He focused his attention on the street prostitutes, those who charged much less and were more anonymous rather than those that advertised online.

"Girls advertise for $1,000 a night - most guys who are serial killers can't afford that," he said.

Rifkin also stated that it was easier to kill prostitutes because they were usually on their backs, so it was much easier to overpower them. Rifkin was unusual compared to other serial killers who targeted prostitutes because he didn't always kill them; some he let go. He often just paid the prostitutes for their company, a temporary friendship of sorts.

He adamantly denied that any of the victims found to date were the result of his handiwork. Considering he was quick to confess to his murders, it's perfectly reasonable to believe he is telling the truth. As mentioned before, Rifkin was cleared as a suspect, but law enforcement says that nobody is completely ruled out.

CHAPTER 11:

LIFE VS. DEATH

There are a lot of people out there who think serial killers like Rifkin should automatically receive the death penalty. After all, why should they get to live when their victims were not given that same opportunity? How could a monster who could take the lives of so many victims be allowed the privilege to live out their lives with no cares in the world? Even life in prison is not really that bad for many of these killers. They have no bills to pay, no families to support, they don't have to go and work a 9 to 5 job, and every meal is prepared and served to them each day.

But there are a lot of reasons why the death penalty is not automatically imposed, the biggest of which is the state in which the trial takes place. Executions were once common throughout the United States, but they have since been abolished in a number of areas.

Pros and Cons

__Death Penalty__

The Pros - Eye for an Eye

The most common argument for the death penalty is the belief that the criminal should experience the same fate as the victim. There is no more severe crime than that of murder, and the feeling of many people is that these murderers don't deserve to live, even if it is behind bars for the rest of their natural life.

This is further fueled by the criminal's ability to lead a fairly normal life, in that they can marry while incarcerated and still have relationships. Whereas the victim no longer has those options, and for the families of the victims, this is often one of the hardest things to live with.

Some see the death penalty as 'an eye for an eye', that the punishment should fit the severity of the crime. The killer shouldn't have the ability to grow old and die a natural death because they don't deserve to.

The Cons - Eye for an Eye

When a murderer is executed, it is sometimes perceived that by killing them, it is just another form of murder. While the premise of an eye for an eye may be satisfying to some, there have been a lot of cases where the wrong person has been executed, then found innocent when it is too late.

Another factor to consider is at what level a murderer should be given the death penalty. Should anyone who kills receive it, or should it only be reserved for those that are classified as serial killers? Inmates have been executed for committing one murder, and this seems rather extreme. Although killing just one person is unacceptable, do they really deserve to die for it? Is that really a case of an eye for an eye when there are often contributing factors to a person killing one victim as opposed to those who murder multiple?

Many think that by executing a killer, it will deter others from killing, but this is just nonsense. The serial killer, for example, is not going to even take into consideration that he or she may die for their crimes. For them, the urge to kill overpowers the threat of death. Rifkin couldn't have stopped, even if he was facing the death penalty.

The Pros - Closure

Executing a killer is considered by many to be a form of closure for the families of the victims. It is also a way to send a message to the families that the judicial system does work, and it works for them as the victims rather than the defendant.

By getting closure for the family, it is similar to the 'eye for an eye' theory. They get the satisfaction of knowing that the person who took the life of their loved one will never be able to do that to anyone else ever again. For some, it is a simple matter of wanting revenge; they killed their family member, therefore they need to die.

The Cons - Closure

To think that by executing a murderer is going to relieve the suffering and bring closure to the family of the victim is nonsense. They may get some benefit of knowing the murderer can't kill anyone else, but it will never take away the grief and anger the families of the victims suffer.

There have been multiple interviews with families of murder victims after an execution where they have stated it doesn't bring any closure for them. Their loved one is still gone, and killing the one who took their life isn't going to bring them back. The feelings of loss and sorrow aren't relieved by the execution of the murderer.

The Pros - Cost of Execution

It seems plausible that by executing a murderer it costs less than it does to incarcerate them for life. The term of incarceration is generally shorter, therefore costing less to house the killer until such time as their execution date arises.

To house and care for each prisoner is expensive, and there are a lot of inmates who are incarcerated at a very young age. So, to keep a prisoner for maybe 60 years until they die is extremely costly, as the state becomes responsible for their meals, medical care, dental, and general costs associated with housing them, such as electricity, water, etc.

The Cons - Cost of Execution

In reality, it is actually more expensive to execute a prisoner in today's society than it is to keep them incarcerated for a life sentence. A hundred years ago, it was more efficient because the executions were carried out extremely quickly, often within a month of the sentence being imposed.

Nowadays though, an inmate with a death sentence can cost up to three times more than it does to house someone for life. Because of the risk of executing an innocent man, the appeals process alone can take decades to complete. Incredibly, many end up dying of natural causes during the lengthy process.

The trials and appeals of convicted murderers are among the most costly of all criminal cases. It can cost an average of more than $2 million in Texas for a death penalty case. This is nearly triple what it costs to keep someone in prison for 40 years.

Life Imprisonment

The Pros - Information Gathering

By keeping a serial killer alive, there are more opportunities for experts and researchers to garner more information about what makes them commit such atrocious murders. When they have the opportunity to talk to these killers, they learn more about their personality, their mental status, and may lead to identifying factors that can all help either prevent serial killing or develop a profile of a potential suspect.

The FBI Behavioral Science Unit conducted numerous interviews with notorious killers such as Ed Kemper and Ted Bundy, and through the knowledge they gained, criminal profiling became a science that has assisted law enforcement all around the world. Without this knowledge, there would be much less understanding about how the mind of a killer works.

The Cons - Information Gathering

Considering the amount of time it takes for a killer to be executed, there would still be plenty of time to talk to them and get any information they are willing to supply. Bundy for example, talked a lot more shortly before he was executed because he knew he was running out of time to say what he wanted to say.

Serial killers are notorious for liking the spotlight, and they go out of their way to take part in as many interviews as they are offered. But the information they give is often of no use. They simply like the sound of their own voice, and they want to be seen as 'important.' This leads to a complete waste of time for all involved, and the killer gets to have his fame increased.

The Pros - Assisting On Cases

At times, investigators have called on the expertise of various serial killers to help with other cases. This is largely based on the belief that serial killers have a tendency to think and act alike; therefore, one may be able to give some insight into an unknown suspect.

Examples include Rifkin, who was asked for his opinions on the Long Island Serial Killer, and Ted Bundy was asked to assist with other serial murder cases before he was executed. They are considered to have relevant knowledge, particularly around how the victims are killed and disposed of.

The Cons - Assisting on Cases

The downside to interviewing serial killers about other cases is twofold. Firstly, no two serial killers are really alike; even copycat killers always do something that is slightly different to the killer they are emulating. There may be similarities in the types of victims targeted or how they are killed, but there will always be a level of difference.

Secondly, serial killers thrive on attention. They enjoy being in the spotlight, so to speak, so there are no guarantees that the information they are giving is accurate or truthful. Often their own stories have gone cold, so it's a way for them to insert themselves back into the minds of the general public.

The Pros - Ongoing Investigations

While a killer is incarcerated for the term of their natural life, it enables investigators to continue with any outstanding cases related to that killer. There may be further victims yet to be discovered, and if the suspect is alive and well, the investigators can go back to them and question their involvement.

This can enable some cases to be resolved, if only to get answers for the family members of the murder victim. The longer a killer is incarcerated, the more likely they are to give out more information as time passes by. They often like to keep some information to themselves to use at a later date, or because it makes them feel they have some sort of power. But eventually, they tend to confess, if only to gain more attention or to use as a bargaining tool.

The Cons - Ongoing Investigations

As with assisting on cases, the information they give is not always the truth, and it can result in a lot of wasted time for the investigators. Not all serial killers will admit to further victims, even though they are seldom charged for them once they have been sentenced to spend their full life behind bars.

Then, of course, there is the cost of housing a prisoner for an extended period of time, especially those who are incarcerated at a fairly young age. Overcrowding is another major issue, and as prisons become fuller, new facilities are required. Overcrowding also leads to other problems, particularly violence among inmates.

Certain types of prisoner, like Rifkin, also require special attention regarding their own safety within the prison. Many killers spend a lot of time in solitary, simply to protect them from others, requiring segregation units to be created in each prison.

The Pros - Killing is Killing

Many of those who oppose the death penalty in favor of life imprisonment believe that execution is no different than murder. Just because someone has killed another person does not necessarily mean that they in turn should die.

Life imprisonment is a deterrent by sending a message to potential killers that murder isn't worth giving up everything in their lives for. A person could kill just one victim and spend the rest of their life behind bars. At least life imprisonment prevents the execution of inmates who are later found to be innocent.

The Cons - Killing is Killing

There are killers out there that commit the most heinous of all murders, and they enjoy it too much. They fear nobody, have no respect for authority, and have no feelings or empathy towards other human beings. If these killers are kept in prison for life instead of being executed, what is to stop them from killing again while incarcerated?

The thought of these types of murderers ever seeing freedom is difficult to bear. Some killers are just so horrendous that they will not stop, and there have been cases of serial killers who continued to murder their fellow inmates, as well as prison guards. The question becomes, does this person deserve to live at the continuous risk of others?

Controversy

One of the most compelling arguments against the death penalty is the number of inmates who were eventually proven to be innocent, sometimes when it was too late. Once the execution has been carried out, it can't be reversed—the person is already dead. So, it is highly critical that innocence or guilt be completely proven before an execution takes place.

There have been 156 death row inmates who were subsequently declared innocent since 1973. Even though the average length of time spent on death row is a little over eleven years, there are cases where the inmate is exonerated years later, but by then, they have already been executed.

Cases of Innocent People Executed

Cameron Todd Willingham

Willingham was convicted in 1992 in Texas for charges of murder and arson. It was alleged he had set a fire that ultimately took the lives of his three children. Willingham was executed in 2004. It was later discovered that the forensic evidence had been misinterpreted, and the fire was actually accidental not intentional.

Larry Griffin

Griffin was found guilty of the murder of Quintin Moss, a drug dealer in Missouri, in 1981. He was executed in 1995, declaring his innocence. It is now believed that an eyewitness gave false testimony, and a second eyewitness was never contacted to give evidence during the trial. The second eyewitness claims Griffin hadn't been at the crime scene the night the murder occurred.

Ruben Cantu

Just 17 years old at the time he was convicted of capital murder, Cantu was executed in 1993 in Texas. Twelve years later, it was discovered that Cantu was most likely innocent of the murder. An eyewitness recanted, and a co-defendant of Cantu's later said he had allowed Cantu to be falsely accused. He also said Cantu hadn't been there at the time of the murder.

Carlos DeLuna

DeLuna was found guilty of stabbing a convenience store clerk to death in Texas and was subsequently executed in 1989. Nearly two decades later, evidence was discovered that he had most likely been innocent and that another man had confessed multiple times to committing the murder.

Jesse Tafero

Tafero was accused and convicted of killing a state trooper in 1976, along with Sonia Jacobs. Both were sentenced to death, and Tafero was executed in 1990. The conviction had been based on the testimony of Walter Rhodes who was involved in the murder, in exchange for Rhodes receiving a life sentence instead of death. In 1992, Jacobs was released from prison due to the lack of evidence—the same evidence that had convicted Tafero.

David Spence

Spence was sentenced to death and subsequently executed in 1997 in Texas. He was convicted of killing three teenagers in what was supposedly a case of mistaken identity. The lead homicide detective and supervising police lieutenant both said that they never had any evidence to prove Spence was involved, and they believed him to have been innocent.

Meeks Griffin and Thomas Griffin

These two brothers were convicted of murder back in 1915. Both black, they had been accused of killing their white victim because another black man Monk Stevenson, also accused of the murder, stated the brothers were responsible. Stevenson later said that the only reason he accused the brothers was because he thought they were wealthy and therefore had the means to beat the criminal charges.

Botched Executions

Another highly controversial aspect of the death penalty is the large number of executions that haven't gone as smoothly as they were meant to. Whether it is by lethal injection, electrocution, or the gas chamber, executions are not always straightforward, and the experience can be just as disturbing for the prisoner as it is for the witness.

Some of the horrible effects of botched executions could be considered undue cruelty. However, there are many that believe that this is just part of what they deserve, as they showed no mercy to their own victims. The pain and torture inflicted by some serial killers on their victims far outweighs the suffering they may experience during an execution that doesn't go to plan.

Botched executions can range from difficulties with IV access for lethal injections to inmates catching on fire in the electric chair. There have been at least 49 cases in America where there has been a major issue during an execution, and these are listed below.

Frank J. Coppola

Virginia, August 10, 1982

Although there have never been specific details released as to what happened during the execution of Coppola, an attorney who was there at the time claimed it took two jolts of electricity lasting 55 seconds each to kill him. With the second jolt, Coppola's leg and head caught on fire, and the smell and sounds of burning flesh were present.

John Evans

Alabama, April 22, 1983

During the execution by electric chair, flames erupted from an electrode attached to his leg after the first jolt of electricity. Sparks and smoke could also be seen coming out from his head, under the hood. Doctors checked and found his heart was still beating, so the electrode was reattached to Evans' leg and another jolt of electricity was sent through his body. More flesh was burned, and yet he still had a heartbeat. His lawyer pleaded with the execution to be halted, but instead a third jolt of electricity was applied. In total the execution took 14 minutes, and Evans' body was burnt and smoldering at the end of it.

Jimmy Lee Gray

Mississippi, September 2, 1983

Gray was sentenced to die in the gas chamber, and within eight minutes of the gas being released, the witnesses had to be cleared from the room because of the grotesque response of his body to the gas. Gray could be seen gasping desperately for air, and his attorney claimed he could be seen banging his head against a metal pole in the chamber. Reporters who were present counted eleven moans coming from Gray. It was later discovered that the man acting as executioner was drunk at the time.

Alpha Otis Stephens

Georgia, December 12, 1984

For six long minutes after the first jolt of electricity, Stephens struggled to breathe. He had received a two minute surge of electricity, and physicians claimed they had to wait for his body to cool down before they could check his heartbeat. He was given a second jolt, which killed him. During the interval between the two jolts, Stephens had taken a total of 23 breaths.

Stephen Peter Morin

Texas, March 13, 1985

It took the execution technicians almost 45 minutes to find a suitable vein to use for the lethal injection. They claimed it was because Morin had a history of being a drug abuser, which had damaged his veins.

William E. Vandiver

Indiana, October 16, 1985

Strapped into the electric chair, Vandiver received 2,300 volts of electricity, after which he was still breathing. He ended up being given five jolts of electricity over 17 minutes before he was declared dead, and his attorney claimed he could smell his flesh burning and there was smoke present. The Department of Corrections admitted something hadn't gone to plan with Vandiver's execution.

Randy Woolls

Texas, August 20, 1986

Like the case of Stephen Morin, Woolls had also been a drug addict, and he ended up having to help the execution technicians find a suitable vein for his lethal injection.

Elliot Rod Johnson

Texas, June 24, 1987

Johnson also suffered from collapsed veins, and because of the difficulty the technicians were having in finding a useable vein, his execution ended up taking almost an hour to complete.

Raymond Landry

Texas, December 13, 1988

Within two minutes of the lethal injection process starting, the syringe came out of his vein, and the chemicals were sprayed across the room towards where the witnesses were seated. Prison officials pulled the curtain between the inmate and the witnesses, and it took another 14 minutes for a catheter to be reinserted. Landry was pronounced dead 24 minutes after the injection began and a total of 40 minutes after he was first strapped to the gurney.

Stephen McCoy

Texas, May 24, 1989

McCoy had a truly horrific physical reaction to the lethal injection. His body was arching up off the gurney, his chest was heaving, and he was gasping and choking for air. One of the witnesses found it so shocking that they fainted, knocking over another witness in the process. The Attorney General of Texas stated that the drugs may have been given in a stronger dose or quicker than usual, resulting in the strong physical reaction McCoy experienced/ endured.

Horace Franklin Dunkins Jr.

Alabama, July 14, 1989

It took 19 minutes for Dunkins to be executed by electric chair. After he was given the first jolt, the prison guard captain stated, "I believe we've got the jacks on wrong." With the jacks improperly attached, the electrical current was not strong enough to cause death. They were reconnected, and a second jolt of electricity was administered. There had been a total of nine minutes between each round of electricity.

Jesse Joseph Tafero

Florida, May 4, 1990

One of the most graphic electrocutions witnessed, at one point during the execution flames as high as six inches were seen erupting from the head of Tafero. It took three jolts of electricity to kill Tafero, and officials claimed human error was responsible for the botched execution. Apparently, a synthetic sponge had been used instead of the normal natural sponge, and a demonstration later showed the synthetic sponge caught fire when exposed to electricity.

Charles Walker

Illinois, September 12, 1990

The execution of Walker by lethal injection was marred by human error and equipment failure, leading to a prolonged and excruciating death. There was apparently a kink in the tube inserted into Walker's arm which prevented the flow of the deadly chemicals. Also, the needle was inserted into his vein so that it was pointing towards his fingers, when it should have been pointing towards his heart.

Wilbert Lee Evans

Virginia, October 17, 1990

As soon as the first jolt of electricity surged through Evans, blood spurted out from under the hood over his face, and his shirt was drenched with it. As blood was dripping from his lips it made a sizzling sound, and Evans was still alive at this point, as he was moaning. A second jolt was applied, and he finally died. On autopsy, it was discovered that his blood pressure, which was normally high, was elevated by the electrical surge and resulted in a bloody nose.

Derick Lynn Peterson

Virginia, August 22, 1991

The prison physician checked for a heartbeat after the first jolt of electricity was administered and declared Peterson was still alive. He waited a further four minutes and checked again, with the same result. A second jolt was then administered, and this time his heart stopped beating. This lead to a decision by officials that for future executions they would administer two rounds of electricity before checking for a heartbeat.

Rickey Ray Rector

Arkansas, January 24, 1992

It took over 50 minutes before medical personnel could find a suitable vein through which to administer the lethal injection to Rector. Witnesses could not see what was happening, but they reported hearing Rector moaning during this time. Rector ended up helping them to find a vein, despite having some level of brain damage. Officials later stated that the difficulty could have been due to his large size and because Rector was on antipsychotic medication.

Donald Eugene Harding

Arizona, April 6, 1992

Harding was executed in the gas chamber, and it took nearly eleven minutes for him to be pronounced dead after the cyanide tablets were dropped. Witnesses say Harding thrashed about violently throughout the execution, and these jerking movements lasted for more than six minutes. Journalist Cameron Harper was a witness that day, and he stated, "Obviously, this man was suffering. This was a violent death... an ugly event. We put animals to death more humanely." Another witness was reporter Carla McClain, who said, "Harding's death was extremely violent. He was in great pain. I heard him gasp and moan. I saw his body turn from red to purple."

Robyn Lee Parks

Oklahoma, March 10, 1992

Within two minutes of being administered the lethal injection, Parks experienced a violent reaction. The muscles in his neck, jaw, and abdomen went into spasms for nearly a minute, and he was gasping and gagging violently for the eleven minutes it took for him to die.

Billy Wayne White

Texas, April 23, 1992

Like others before, there were a lot of difficulties finding a suitable vein for the lethal injection. This was put down to White having a history of abusing heroin. It took 47 minutes from the time he was strapped to the gurney for White to die.

Justin Lee May

Texas, May 7, 1992

During his execution by lethal injection, May reportedly coughed, gasped, and struggled against his restraints. It was a violent reaction to the drugs, and May groaned and lifted his head off the gurney, having major coughing spasms. After he died, his mouth and eyes were still open.

John Wayne Gacy

Illinois, May 10, 1994

Serial killer Gacy was administered the lethal injection, but shortly after it was given, the chemicals solidified, blocking the IV tube. A second tube was inserted, and the process was resumed ten minutes later. It took 18 minutes for the execution to be successful. It was reported that the issue with the IV was due to human error, that the officials conducting the execution were inexperienced.

Emmitt Foster

Missouri, May 3, 1995

After being administered the lethal injection, the execution was stopped seven minutes into the process because the lethal chemicals had ceased circulating. Foster convulsed and gasped, and the curtains were drawn so the witnesses couldn't see what was going on. Half an hour later, Foster was pronounced deceased, and only then were the curtains opened again, leaving the witnesses to view his corpse. The coroner identified that the problem was caused by the straps holding Foster to the gurney. They were discovered to be so tight that they restricted the flow of the chemicals, so he entered the chamber and instructed the officials to loosen the straps so the execution could be successful.

Richard Townes Jr.

Virginia, January 23, 1996

This was another case where the medical personnel were unable to find a vein that was big enough to be suitable for the size of the lethal injection needle. After numerous failed attempts, the needle was eventually inserted through the top of Townes's foot.

Tommie J. Smith

Indiana, July 18, 1996

The execution team attempted to find a suitable vein for 16 minutes, at which point a physician was called in to assist. The physician administered a local anesthetic and tried to insert the IV into Smith's neck, which also failed. Finally an angio-catheter was inserted in his foot, 49 minutes after the first attempt. The witnesses were then allowed to view the actual execution, and it took another 20 minutes for Smith's heart to stop. In total, it had taken 1 hour and 9 minutes.

Pedro Medina

Florida, March 25, 1997

This was yet another visually horrifying electrocution that went wrong. As the first round of electricity was administered to Medina, flames measuring a foot in height shot up from the headpiece. The air was filled with smoke and the stench of burning flesh, and it was so bad that the witnesses present gagged. One of the officials cut off the power supply manually by throwing a switch before the full two minute cycle of voltage had completed. Medina's chest heaved until the flames went out and his heart stopped. It was later concluded that the flames resulted from improper placement of the sponge on Medina's head, which was used to conduct the electricity.

Scott Dawn Carpenter

Oklahoma, May 8, 1997

Following the administration of the lethal injection, Carpenter gasped for air, his body spasmed, and a guttural sound was exerted from him. His body stopped moving after three minutes, and he was pronounced dead eleven minutes after the injection was administered.

Michael Eugene Elkins

South Carolina, June 13, 1997

Elkins suffered from liver disease and problems with his spleen, leaving his body badly swollen. This made it difficult to source a suitable vein for the lethal injection, and after multiple failed attempts, an IV was inserted into a neck vein.

Joseph Cannon

Texas, April 23, 1998

Cannon was administered the lethal injection, and almost

immediately, the vein in his arm holding the needle collapsed, and the needle popped out. The curtain was closed to block the view of the witnesses, and another attempt to find a good vein was made. When the curtain was opened 15 minutes later, Cannon was weeping, and after making a second final statement, the execution was carried out.

Genaro Ruiz Camacho

Texas, August 26, 1998

Just like many before him, Camacho also suffered from poor veins. There was a delay of almost two hours before the execution was completed, largely due to the difficulty of finding a suitable vein through which to administer the lethal injection.

Roderick Abeyta

Nevada, October 5, 1998

Another death row inmate with poor veins, it took the execution team 25 minutes to insert the needle properly, and then the lethal injection was administered.

Allen Lee Davis

Florida, July 8, 1999

A new electric chair had been built to accommodate larger death row inmates, and Davis was the first to be strapped into it. During the execution, blood poured from his nose and mouth, saturating his shirt collar and spreading to the size of a dinner plate on his chest. It was commented later that the execution of Davis looked as though he had been tortured brutally. The photos of the execution were circulated widely by internet and are incredibly graphic.

Christina Marie Riggs

Arkansas, May 3, 2000

Prison staff spent 18 minutes trying to insert a needle into her elbow for the lethal injection before she agreed to let them insert the needle into her wrist. Interestingly, Riggs had dropped her appeals and requested execution.

Bennie Demps

Florida, June 8, 2000

The protocol in Florida for lethal injections is that there must be two separate lines inserted. The execution team had no trouble inserting one needle but struggled to insert the second. After trying for more than 30 minutes, they gave up, and the execution was allowed to go ahead. When Demps made his final statement, he said they had cut him in the leg and the groin, and that he was bleeding profusely. He claimed it wasn't an execution but a murder.

Claude Jones

Texas, December 7, 2000

The execution of Jones was delayed by half an hour as the team struggled to gain intravenous access. Jones had been a drug abuser, and after failing to insert the needle five times, the executioners were finally able to find a good vein in the calf of his leg. Because of the fragility of the veins and the difficulty they had finding one they could use, the lethal injection drugs had to be administered more slowly than usual.

Bert Leroy Hunter

Missouri, June 28, 2000

Hunter reacted badly to the lethal injection and was gasping and coughing before he fell unconscious. He reportedly suffered violent convulsions repeatedly, but not all witnesses agreed that this had occurred.

Jose High

Georgia, November 7, 2001

An hour and nine minutes after the lethal injection began, High was pronounced dead. It took nearly 20 minutes for the contracted medical technicians to find a vein that was suitable, and they abandoned all efforts. Finally a needle was inserted into High's hand, and a physician who was called in was able to insert a second needle between his neck and shoulder.

Joseph L. Clark

Ohio, May 2, 2006

Technicians took 22 minutes to insert the lethal injection needle, and just a few minutes into the process, the vein collapsed. This resulted in his arm swelling, and he lifted up his head and said, "It don't work. It don't work." He said this five times, before the curtains were closed, and the technicians spent an additional 30 minutes locating another vein. Witnesses stated they could hear Clark moaning and crying out, as well as making guttural noises, before he was declared dead. It had taken 90 minutes from start to finish.

Angel Diaz

Florida, December 13, 2006

After he received the first injection, Diaz was still moving, his face grimacing as he tried to speak. A second dose was administered, and it took 34 minutes before he was declared deceased. During his autopsy, the medical examiner found that the IV catheters had gone right through his veins, so the lethal chemicals were injected into the soft tissue instead of the blood. Within two days of the execution, the Governor suspended all executions in Florida temporarily while a commission investigated the safety and humanity of lethal injections.

Christopher Newton

Ohio, May 24, 2007

Medical staff from the prison had difficulty finding suitable veins in Newton's arms for the lethal injection. It took at least ten attempts at inserting needles, and Newton was declared dead nearly two hours after the process had begun.

John Hightower

Georgia, June 26, 2007

The execution of Hightower took 59 minutes, after medical nurses took 40 minutes to find a suitable vein for the lethal injection.

Curtis Osborne

Georgia, June 4, 2008

Osborne's execution had already been delayed for 55 minutes while the Supreme Court reviewed his last appeal, when prison medical staff began trying to insert needles for the lethal injection. It took another 35 minutes to find a suitable vein. Osborne was declared dead 14 minutes after the chemicals were injected.

Romell Broom

Ohio, September 15, 2009

After two hours of trying to find a suitable vein, the execution was terminated. During the multiple attempts, Broom at one point sobbed into his hands in pain. The Governor ordered the execution to be halted and rescheduled for a week's time so that a consultation could take place with physicians as to the best way to execute Broom. He has still not been executed and is on death row.

Brandon Joseph Rhode

Georgia, September 27, 2010

The execution was initially postponed for six days after Rhode attempted suicide using a razor blade he had been given by a guard. On the day of his execution, it took half an hour to find a suitable vein. He was declared deceased 14 minutes after the lethal injection was administered.

Dennis McGuire

Ohio, January 16, 2014

McGuire was administered midazolam and hydromorphone during his execution, and for 25 minutes, he gasped for air as the drugs slowly started to work. He was reported to have made snorting sounds and choking noises while struggling and clenching his fist. His family filed a lawsuit for the pain he appeared to be suffering, claiming he looked like he had suffocated to death.

Clayton D. Lockett

Oklahoma, April 29, 2014

There had been numerous warnings and legal concerns about using the drug midazolam for lethal injections, but the execution of Lockett and fellow inmate Charles Warner was scheduled to go ahead as planned. Lockett was first on the agenda, and it took an hour to find a vein that was suitable, finally located in Lockett's groin. The first drug administered was the sedative, and ten minutes later, the supervising physician announced Lockett was unconscious, which was necessary before the next two drugs were administered, as doing so while a person was conscious would be excruciatingly painful. However, three minutes after they were administered, it became clear that Lockett was still conscious, and he writhed around, clenching his teeth, heavily breathing, and trying to lift up his head. The curtains were lowered so the witnesses couldn't see, and a quarter of an hour later, they were instructed to leave. The execution was halted 20 minutes after the first drug had been administered, and a two-week stay of execution was ordered. However, Lockett suffered a heart attack 43 minutes after the start of the execution and died in the chamber.

Joseph R. Wood

Arizona, July 23, 2014

Wood also received the drugs midazolam and hydromorphone during his lethal injection. After the drugs were administered, Wood gasped repeatedly for 1 hour and 40 minutes before he was pronounced deceased. During the execution, his lawyers filed an emergency appeal to the Federal District Court and called the Supreme Court Justice in an effort to halt the execution, but they were unsuccessful. One of the witnesses, reporter Michael Kiefer, claimed that Wood had gasped 640 times before he died.

Brian Keith Terrell

The assigned nurse took more than an hour to insert the required needles into Terrell for the lethal injection. Eventually, she managed to insert one needle into his right hand, and during the attempts Terrell was seen wincing in pain.

Brandon Jones

Georgia, February 3, 2016

Jones was 72 years old at the time of his execution, which probably contributed to the difficulty the execution team had with trying to insert needles into his veins. They spent 24 minutes trying to get a needle into his left arm and then spent a further 8 minutes trying on his right arm. Still unsuccessful, they then tried the left arm again. Eventually, they asked a physician for help, and another 13 minutes were spent inserting the needle into Jones' groin and suturing it in place.

Ronald Bert Smith Jr.

Alabama, December 8, 2016

After Smith was administered the lethal injection chemicals, he coughed, gasped, and struggled to breathe for 13 minutes. He was observed clenching his fists and lifting his head during the process. He was pronounced dead 34 minutes after the execution began. One of the drugs used during the execution was the controversial midazolam.

Summary

It may not seem such a big deal to many if the condemned man had to undergo a bit of pain or distress due to difficulties experienced throughout numerous attempts at inserting needles and catheters, especially when it is compared to the suffering they inflicted on their victims, but the law protects even the condemned, requiring executions to be carried out in a humane manner. It is not lawful or constitutional to cause undue suffering and torture, even during a legal execution.

The failure to insert a needle is quite different from some of the more severe reactions experienced during many of these executions. While it seems that the lethal injection has caused the majority of complications, those which resulted from the electric chair appear to be more severe. Flames shooting out from the body, bleeding, and even smoke coming from under the execution hood are all hard to imagine a human being enduring.

As time goes on, executions are becoming more and more controversial, particularly regarding lethal injections and the drugs used. It seems almost strange that a killer can take the life of another person in a quick and efficient manner, yet the State cannot do the same.

What does this mean for Rifkin? It means he really has dodged a bullet, so to speak. He is lucky that he gets to live his life out in prison rather than face the daunting prospect of meeting the same fate as his victims. With the number of things going wrong with executions, even recently, there could have been a chance that Rifkin may have been one of these statistics of botched executions that were botched. Is this fair that he gets to live? That is a question that only an individual can answer.

CHAPTER 12:

THE IMPACT OF MOVIES AND RIFKIN MEDIA

It has long been queried whether movies and media really have an impact on the instigation of murders. There have been plenty of cases where parents, authorities, and the public have blamed a particular movie or rock song for damaging the minds of their children, leading to violent acts. But is it really a case of them mimicking what they see and hear, or does it depend on the psychological makeup of the person in the first place?

Frenzy

Throughout his assessments and interviews, Rifkin has always alluded that his fantasies of prostitutes and murder were triggered by the movie 'Frenzy' by Alfred Hitchcock. Referring to it as his favorite movie, Rifkin states that it was while watching this movie that he first got the idea to strangle prostitutes, and when he was stuck with a dead body in a motel, the inspiration to purchase a steamer trunk to remove the body also came from Frenzy.

Frenzy was produced in 1972, and is a well-known British

thriller—one that many suggest was the best movie of Hitchcock's career. Based on a novel, the plot focuses on a serial killer in London, and during one of the earlier scenes, the serial killers Christie and Jack the Ripper are mentioned.

The serial killer in the movie rapes and strangles women with neckties, with most of the film taking place in Covent Garden, a flourishing fruit and vegetable market at the time. As the plot unfolds, the main character, the killer, is seen dragging a large trunk up a staircase for the purpose of removing a corpse.

The movie is largely described as being darkly humorous and suspenseful, and for some people, disturbing. It was more overtly sexual than Hitchcock's other films, and the violence more brutal. The murder of Brenda Blaney in the film shows a close-up of her face as she is raped and strangled to death.

When Rifkin appears on videotaped interviews, his face tends to change when he talks about the movie. It's almost as though he can see the scenes running through his head while he's thinking about them. 'Frenzy' clearly made a very strong impact on Rifkin, most likely because he was already having disturbing thoughts at the time that he didn't fully comprehend, and because it was at this time when he became isolated and lonely.

Some may wonder if it was the close-up of the face when the character was murdered that affected Rifkin so much. However, when he was asked about looking into the faces of his victims as he killed them, he said that he often looked away, just wanting the whole process to be over. Of the times he thought he may have looked at their faces, he couldn't recall having any particular feelings as they died.

Cases of Murder Mimicking Media

Following are cases where murders seem to have mimicked different forms of media, from movies to television shows and books.

Television Shows

Breaking Bad

This was a highly successful and popular television series about a high school chemistry teacher who makes and sells drugs to pay for medical treatment. Potential copycat case:

- Jason Hart, 27, was convicted of strangling his girlfriend and disposing of her body in a plastic tub and covering the body with sulfuric acid.
  - Scenes in 'Breaking Bad' showed the characters disposing of bodies in a similar way. Hart was a fan of the show.

Movies

Scream

A well-known series of horror movies, the basis of 'Scream' was a man running around in a Ghostface costume stabbing people to death.

- Thierry Jaradin, 24, was convicted of stabbing a young girl Alisson Cambier in a similar way experienced by the victims in the movie. Cambier was stabbed 30 times. He had been wearing the Ghostface mask at the time of the murder and stated he had planned it to be similar to the movie.

The Dark Knight

The popular Batman movie has been considered to be the impetus for a number of violent crimes, including murder.

- James Holmes entered a movie theatre in Aurora in 2012, and opened fire on the audience. He killed 12 innocent movie-goers, and when he was arrested, he claimed to be 'the Joker.'
- A Wisconsin man dressed as the Joker assaulted his girlfriend and cousin in 2010 when he found them sleeping together.
- In 2009, a teacher was attacked by a young girl who had painted her face to resemble the Joker.

Saw

This particularly horrifying movie left many with nightmares and is the epitome of a psychological thriller.

- Two teenage boys were reported in Salt Lake City for being heard planning to kidnap, torture, and murder people.

They were overheard saying they were going to teach some people a lesson for hurting others. They had gone so far as to set cameras up so they could record the murders but were foiled before they could go through with it.

- Matthew Tinling, 25, copied a torture scene from 'Saw VI', torturing his neighbor to obtain the PIN for his bank account. He stabbed his victim 17 times in the neck, legs, and head, and tried to sever his spinal cord.

American Psycho/Silence of the Lambs

Both of these horror movies were wildly popular, but for one killer in particular, they had an even bigger impact.

- Michael Hernandez, 14, stabbed his friend to death after luring him into the bathroom at school. He inflicted 40 wounds and later said he identified with the horror movie murderers and wanted to act them out. He aspired to become a serial killer.

Natural Born Killers

A movie featuring Woody Harrelson, it depicts the story of a young couple traveling the roads and murdering people who crossed their paths.

- Dylan Klebold and Eric Harris were the perpetrators of the Columbine Massacre, a rampage that only ended with their suicides. They were fans of the movie and made numerous mentions of it in diaries and written notes.

- Sarah Edmondson and Ben Darras went on a mission to mimic the killing spree acted out in the movie. They shot and killed the owner of a liquor store in March 1995, then shot a store clerk, who survived, a few days later.

The Collector

Originally a book, the movie is the story of a butterfly-collecting nobody with an admiration for a student called Miranda, but who doesn't have the social skills to form a relationship. He eventually kidnaps her and holds her captive.

- Serial killer Leonard Lake kidnapped Kathy Allen and Brenda O'Connor and kept them in a bunker where he raped and tortured them along with his partner Charles Ng. Lake had given the name 'Operation Miranda' to his plans to kidnap and kill.
- Robert Berdella, another serial killer, said 'The Collector' had inspired him to abduct and imprison several men, of whom he then photographed as he tortured before they were murdered. He said the movie made a 'lasting impression' on him.

Halloween

'Halloween' is a horror movie featuring the character 'Michael Myers' who wears a mask and commits multiple slashing murders.

- In 2012, teenager Jake Evans murdered his mother and sister inside their home in Texas. When he confessed to the murders, he stated he had watched 'Halloween' three times that week and was amazed at how the killer had been calm during the murders and showed very little guilt afterwards. Evans said he thought it would feel the same way if he killed someone.

Queen of the Damned

This movie centered on a character called Akasha who was a vampire.

- Allan Menzies murdered Thomas McKendrick by stabbing him 42 times, in Edinburgh. He said he had watched the movie more than 100 times, and he had been ordered to kill by the character Akasha. After he had killed McKendrick, he drank his blood and ate part of the young man's skull.

<u>Copycat Killers</u>

Zodiac Killer

Though not a media as such, there was so much information reported about the unsolved case of the Zodiac killer that it was relatively easy for a copycat to mimic the crimes.

- Eddie Seda killed victims in New York City in the 1980s in a similar way to the Zodiac's method of murder. He also left notes at each crime scene, like Zodiac, and sent cryptic letters to law enforcement. He was caught due to leaving his fingerprints on the notes.

Jack the Ripper

It is not terribly surprising that there have been killers who have tried to copy the crimes of the Ripper. It is one of the greatest unsolved mysteries known, and perhaps the copycat wanted to try and be as clever as the Ripper, by not being identified.

- Derek Brown, 48, killed two young women—a street vendor and a prostitute. They were murdered in a manner similar to the Ripper's methods, but their bodies were never found. It's believed Brown dismembered them in his bathtub before disposing of them.

Items of Media Regarding Rifkin

- Rifkin was mentioned during the 'Criminal Minds' episode 'Charm and Harm'. He was used as an example of a killer who had used the ruse of being a photographer.
- In the television series 'Seinfeld', the episode 'The Masseuse' introduced a boyfriend of the character Elaine as being called Joel Rifkin. The serial killer is referenced many times during the episode. At one point, the name Joel Rifkin is announced at a New York Giant's game over the loudspeaker, and he decides that Elaine was right about suggesting he change his name.

Murderabilia

- A letter and envelope in Rifkin's handwriting is available for sale on one of the many Murderabilia websites for $375. In comparison, a letter and envelope written by Aileen Wuornos on the same site is only worth $225.
- A handmade Valentines card on another site is listed for sale in the amount of $500.
- In April 1998, Rifkin contributed some of his artwork to an inmate art show being displayed at the New York State legislature office in Albany. Twenty of his sketches and paintings were for sale, most depicting wildlife and flowers, but one in particular caused a considerable amount of outrage. Titled 'Guardian's Failure', the painting showed a human foot with a toe tag and in the corner of the painting was an angel weeping.

Trivia

- Rifkin announced in August 1999 that he had plans to open a shelter for prostitutes that he would call 'Oholah House.' The plan included medical care, drug treatment, job training, and counseling. He chose the name 'Oholah', a Hebrew word which means 'sanctuary' because it is also the name of a prostitute whose murder was described in Ezekiel 23:3-10.

Rifkin said this was his way of 'paying back a debt.' There were a number of people who thought it was a good idea, including the prosecutor Fred Klein. But, one part of the plan sparked a lot of objection. Rifkin planned to incorporate what he called a 'motivation room', where the prostitutes would be shown photos of murdered prostitutes in an effort to scare them straight. Rifkin said, "These girls think, 'I can't be touched'. Well, 17 girls thought that, and now they're dead."

- Quote by Rifkin, "I will in all probability be convicted, but I will not go away as a monster but as a tragedy."
- The home Rifkin had shared with his mother and his sister Jan was sold in 2011, following the death of his mother. Despite the horrible history of the house—it was where Rifkin had killed and dismembered some of his victims—the buyers were not put off, and the sale went through.

David 'Insurgent' Rubinstein

Despite all of his personal issues, it was the actions of Rifkin that instigated the suicide of David 'Insurgent' Rubinstein.

Rubinstein had been the co-founder and lead singer of a hardcore punk band called 'Reagan Youth' in New York. Still in school at the time, the band played at a number of punk clubs in Manhattan and a variety of other venues. They never recorded a single, but self-published tapes and albums which reached substantially high sales levels.

The band was a 'left-wing anti-racist' group that often portrayed

Nazi and Ku Klux Klan imagery as forms of political satire during their shows. By the end of the 1980s, the members of the band were worn out after years of touring, not making enough money, and drug addiction. They disbanded at the same time as Ronald Reagan left the Whitehouse.

Rubinstein was seriously addicted to heroin by the time they disbanded and had taken to dealing drugs to survive. He met Tiffany Bresciani, who was working as a stripper and a prostitute at the time. She used the money she received from being a prostitute to finance their drug habits. Often, Rubinstein would wait for her while she was with a client, then they would go together to buy drugs.

Rubinstein and Bresciani were standing on Allen Street on June 24, 1993, waiting for a customer when someone she had met before pulled up. Bresciani got into the familiar Mazda truck and told Rubinstein she would be back in 20 minutes. When she didn't return, Rubinstein called the police and gave them a description of the truck. It was a few days later that Bresciani's body was found in the back of Rifkin's truck.

Within a week of Bresciani's death, Rubinstein was deeply depressed over the loss of his girlfriend, and it was compounded by the death of his mother around the same time. He committed suicide on July 3, 1993, by drug overdose.

This was a prime example of just how much the murder of a loved one can affect those left behind. When killers like Rifkin murder a victim, not a second thought is ever given about the family and friends of that victim and how they are going to be affected. Serial killers are considered by many people to be the most selfish human beings, only interested in satisfying their own urges without a care for anyone else.

CONCLUSION

Rifkin not only took away the lives of his many victims, but he also forever changed the lives of the family members, friends, and work colleagues of the victims as well. The number of people affected by a murder is far higher than just the immediate family. Even hardened, experienced, law enforcement officers can be greatly affected by the tragedy of murder, which then can affect their own families. Murder is a far-reaching tragedy that spirals out from the victim to encompass anyone who knew them, loved them, or was brought into the process through medical and law authorities.

Like all other serial killers, Rifkin never gave a single thought about those he killed and those left behind. He showed no mercy, no remorse, and no empathy. His only concerns were of his own cravings and need to take the lives of these women, some of whom he had known for quite some time.

Rifkin claims he doesn't know why he killed so many women, and this may indeed be the case. But it is more likely that he has some insight into his own thoughts and feelings. Otherwise, he would have killed them all instead of letting some go free unharmed. This shows that he was capable of stopping himself;

he simply chose not to kill on some occasions.

The only small satisfaction for those affected by the murderous actions of Rifkin is that he will never be allowed to go free. He will remain in prison until he dies, unable to take the lives of any other women, having to live by strict rules and regulations to prevent him from inflicting any further pain on the community.

The science is not quite there yet to prevent serial killers from existing, and there is still a lot of work to be done to understand what makes them kill, or what potential treatments or therapies could be employed to further reduce the risk. Unfortunately, men like Rifkin have prowled the earth for centuries, and they will most likely continue to wreak havoc and horror for centuries to come.

More Books By Jack Rosewood

There is little more terrifying than those who hunt, stalk and snatch their prey under the cloak of darkness. These hunters search not for animals, but for the touch, taste, and empowerment of human flesh. They are cannibals, vampires and monsters, and they walk among us.

These serial killers are not mythical beasts with horns and shaggy hair. They are people living among society, going about their day to day activities until nightfall. They are the Dennis Rader's, the fathers, husbands, church going members of the community.

This A-Z encyclopedia of 150 serial killers is the ideal reference book. Included are the most famous true crime serial killers, like Jeffrey Dahmer, John Wayne Gacy, and Richard Ramirez, and not to mention the women who kill, such as Aileen Wuornos and Martha Rendell. There are also lesser known serial killers, covering many countries around the world, so the range is broad.

Each of the serial killer files includes information on when and how they killed the victims, the background of each killer, or the suspects in some cases such as the Zodiac killer, their trials and punishments. For some there are chilling quotes by the killers themselves. The Big Book of Serial Killers is an easy to follow collection of information on the world's most heinous murderers.

You don't want to miss this story about one of the worst serial killer duos in American history.

California has spawned some of America's most notorious serial killers—The "Grim Sleeper" Lonnie Franklin Junior, the "Night Stalker" Richard Ramirez, and Randy Kraft are just three of the Golden State's most notable—which has brought the state some unwanted and some would say unwarranted attention. For its part, California is the most populous state in the U.S., so it would stand to reason that it would have more than its fair share of serial killers. But the state does seem to breed its own special blend of sociopaths.

Far from the glitz and glamour of Los Angles or the scenic backdrops of the Bay Area, two men embarked on a vicious campaign in California's Central Valley that left at least twenty people dead. The two men—Wesley Shermantine and Loren Herzog—became collectively known by law enforcement as the

"Speed Freak Killers" because the duo were almost always under the influence of the drug crystal methamphetamine when they committed several strings of murders during the 1980s and '90s. Herzog and Shermantine were known to be avid outdoorsmen who hunted and fished for various game, but when the two men were high on meth, they focused their attention on hunting the ultimate game—humans.

Open the pages of the following book and learn the complete story of the Speed Freak Killers, Wesley Shermantine and Loren Herzog. You will learn about the early lives of the two men and how they evolved from local toughs into one of the most efficiently dangerous serial killer pairs in American history. The Speed Freak Killers' odyssey of murder continued for nearly twenty years and in many ways continues on until the present. So open the book if you dare to learn about one of the most notorious serial killer tandems ever known

In this gruesome true crime anthology you will read about twelve true crime stories that baffled investigators and continue to draw interest among the public due to their shocking details. From tragic cases of spousal murder to tragic cases of child murder, this true crime book will surely keep your attention.

Three cases of spousal homicide are among the many murder stories in this volume that will keep you captivated. Read about how two wives, Larissa Schuster and Susan Wright, decided to kill their husbands for greed and about how a husband and father, John Sharpe, decided he did not want to be married anymore, so he killed his wife and daughter. For different reasons, these killers thought that they would get away with their crimes, but the ensuing criminal investigations revealed their evil plans for the world to see.

This volume also features a number of child abduction cases that unfortunately ended in tragedy. Follow the course of these true murder cases and learn how the investigators worked tirelessly to put these monsters behind bars. You will also be introduced to cases that can only be described as strange or weird, such as the case of Donald Webb, who was a master of multiple identities and Vlado Taneski, a journalist who created his own scoops through murder. This may be a true crime book, but you are guaranteed to be at the edge of your seat and will probably think at times that you are actually reading a true crime novel.

GET THESE BOOKS FOR FREE

Go to **www.jackrosewood.com**
and get these E-Books for free!

A NOTE FROM THE AUTHOR

Hello, this is Jack Rosewood. Thank you for reading this book. I hope you enjoyed the read. If you did, I'd appreciate if you would take a few moments to post a review.

I would also love if you'd sign up to my newsletter to receive updates on new releases, promotions and a FREE copy of my Herbert Mullin E-Book, www.JackRosewood.com/free

Thanks again for reading this book, make sure to follow me on Facebook.

Best Regards

Jack Rosewood